A Soldier's Tale
A Newfoundland Soldier in Afghanistan

Jamie MacWhirter

Library and Archives Canada Cataloguing in Publication

MacWhirter, Jamie
A soldier's tale : a Newfoundland soldier in Afghanistan /
Jamie MacWhirter.

ISBN 978-1-926689-55-5

1. MacWhirter, Jamie. 2. MacWhirter, Jamie--Mental health.
3. Afghan War, 2001- --Personal narratives, Canadian. 4. Soldiers-
-Newfoundland and Labrador--Biography. 5. Canada. Canadian
Armed Forces. Service Battalion, 1--Biography. 6. Afghan war,
2001- --Psychological aspects. 7. Post-traumatic stress disorder.
I. Title.

DS371.413.M32 2013   958.104'7092   C2013-900168-9

Printed in Canada in 2013
Design and layout by Colin Noseworthy
Front Cover: Photo courtesy of U.S. Army (www.flickr.com)
Back Cover: Photo supplied by author

We acknowledge the financial support of the
Government of Canada through the Canada Book
Fund for our publishing activities

We acknowledge the financial support of the
Government of Newfoundland and Labrador through
the Department of Tourism, Culture and Recreation
for our publishing activities.

Dedication

I would like to dedicate this book to my wonderful wife Vanessa. When I was lost in the darkness of anger you were the light that showed me the way home. I love you.

Jamie

Table of Contents

Walter 1

A Soldier's Tale 5

Message From The Author 7

About Jamie. 8

My Story 15

After The Tour .225

Anger 242

Love and Marriage 246

Epilogue. 251

Jamie's Photo Album. 254

Private Hugh McWhirter, the Regiment's first fatal casualty in action, is buried in Half to Cemetery, Santa Bay. (Photograph of grave by C. S. Frost)

Walter

When I was a kid I remember being told a story about Dad's uncles, Hugh Walter and George McWhirter (some family members use this spelling), from Humbermouth, Bay of Islands. I especially remember Walter because he and I shared the same birth date, March 18th.

Walter was no stranger to hard times. In 1914, at age 19, he went sealing aboard the SS *Newfoundland* and he was there when a terrible tragedy took place. The story of the SS *Newfoundland* seal hunting disaster is one that is familiar to just about everyone in Newfoundland and Labrador.

On March 30, 1914, out in the North Atlantic ice fields, 166 sealers left the *Newfoundland*, which was jammed in ice, and headed towards the SS *Stephano*, seven miles away, which had found a herd of seals. They went anticipating a good day hunting seals. A group of 34 men turned back as the weather worsened, but the remaining men pressed on. When they reached the *Stephano*, Captain Abram

Kean invited them onboard for a lunch of tea and hard bread. Afterwards, Kean navigated the ship towards a herd of seals to the south and ordered the men to kill 1,500 seals before returning to the *Newfoundland*, which was skippered by his son, Westbury Kean. For the next two days, the 132 sealers were stranded on the ice in blizzard conditions and without adequate shelter. The younger Kean believed the men were aboard his father's ship while the father believed the men had made it safely back to the *Newfoundland*. There was no way of communicating between ships as the *Newfoundland* was not equipped with wireless equipment.

It was not until April 2 that Westbury Kean saw his men crawling and staggering on the ice. A total of 77 men had died on the ice, but rescuers found only 69 bodies, the remaining eight had likely fallen into the water. The survivors were brought to St. John's where another man, John Keels, died as the result of his ordeal on the ice.

Young Hugh Walter McWhirter was among those who made it safely back. He returned home to find his brother George had signed up for the army. This came as a surprise to Walter because George was too young to join. But he soon found out that George had lied about his age so that he could go and fight for his country in World War One.

Without a second thought Walter decided to join the army as well, figuring that way he could keep an eye on his little brother. George was Number 846 in the Newfoundland Regiment. Walter was Number 902. The brothers stayed together all through their training overseas, always looking out for each other and having each other's back. They wrote letters home telling where they had been and what they had done. The brothers were shipped to Gallipoli for their first war engagement in August 1915. They arrived in Suvla Bay on September 18. Just days later, on September 22, Walter was killed by a Turkish shell. He was 21.

I was told George witnessed the death of his brother, but had to soldier on without him. I can't imagine the horror of seeing your own brother killed right before your eyes and you having to keep going on without him. George's left arm was shattered by a piece of trench mortar on December 3, 1917, in the Battle of Cambrai, and he ended up being captured by the Germans and sent to a prisoner of war camp where he spent nine months. I was told the Germans took his blood for their own wounded and broke his legs so it would be impossible for him to escape.

George made it home after the war but he was never the same. My father and uncles told me stories of how George did nothing but drink all day when he was back in Newfoundland. If he wasn't drinking, he was fighting. He would fight anyone who crossed him. Sometimes, it was members of his family like his other brother, Pete, my grandfather.

I remember a story about Mr. Ryan who lived next door to my grandfather. Mr. Ryan had a long white picket fence that ran along by his beautiful garden. One day George walked along by the white picket fence and as he passed each picket he would punch it and break it. He broke every single picket.

My father told me that you could pass by George's house at night and hear him yelling or crying in his sleep. Just like me, after I returned from Afghanistan, he suffered from nightmares.

I was told George never wanted to talk about the war and I didn't understand why. I thought he would want to tell his stories to show people how tough and brave he was. But now that I am older I understand. It's not about bragging or trying to show people what you can do when you have to. George didn't want to tell the stories because when you tell the stories you often re-live what happened, and coming from a soldier's point of view a lot of what you go through you want to forget. Maybe that's why I hate head doctors so much. Every time I had to go see mine it was like I had to re-live something terrible that I went through when all I wanted to do was forget it and move on with my life.

A Soldier's Tale

A soldier's tale. You know, when I first looked at those words on paper I thought the same thing I bet most of you think of when you read them. I thought about a story of someone on a battlefield with bullets flying around their head and the whistling sound as the metal cut through the air; how the ground shakes when an artillery round hits; the eerie sound a tank vehicle makes as it approaches and the closer it gets the louder it gets.

I think that is the story most of us know when it comes to a soldier's tale. But what about the other side of the story? When a soldier leaves for a tour of duty what about loved ones left at home, sons and daughters, who worry if their father or mother will return home safely? How about parents who worry and wonder if they will ever see their child again? No matter how old that soldier is a mother still sees her child. And how about the soldier's spouse or sweetheart? This is someone left with so many responsibilities it's hard to know where to begin. The spouse pays the bills, does all the housework plus the yard work. If it's the winter the spouse shovels the driveway and cooks dinner. The spouse washes the clothes and does the dishes. If there is a baby, the spouse changes all the diapers.

Or how about a tale of how the soldier tries to fit into a normal life after returning home. Because, you see, not all wounds are physical, most are mental, and when a soldier gets injured mentally the wound takes a lot longer to heal.

A soldier spends the whole time overseas thinking about home, thinking about friends and family. But when the soldier is over there he or she doesn't think about how things change even over a short period of time like six to nine months. On top of that, when family and friends back home think about the soldier it is about how he or she was before they left. They don't think about how the soldier has changed. So when the soldier returns and sees that things are not the way he or she remembers the soldier becomes confused and angry. When family and friends see that that the soldier is different they ask questions and say 'Hey, you've changed.' When this kind of situation occurs a soldier does not think. A soldier simply reacts. The problem is that the soldier's reaction always involves anger.

So I wanted to tell a soldier's story from all the angles. I wanted readers to see the full effect war can have on not just soldiers, but entire families. War doesn't end on a battlefield. It ends when the soldier finds peace again.

Message From The Author

In 2006, I served my country in Afghanistan with an amazing group of people I consider my brothers. While I was over there I kept a journal of everything that happened either to me or one of my fellow brothers.

The story you are about to read is based on this journal and on my personal life.

Author Jamie MacWhirter is a career soldier. He joined the 2nd Royal Newfoundland Regiment in Corner Brook when he was in his teens. He went on to serve with 1st Service Battalion, an Edmonton-based deployable field unit of the Canadian Forces, and did a tour of duty in Afghanistan in 2006. He is currently station dispatcher with Canadian Forces Station in St. John's.

About Jamie

Before we get into my story let me take some time to tell you a little about myself. My name is Jamie MacWhirter and I was born in Corner Brook, Newfoundland, in the year 1976. I stand six feet tall with blue eyes and brown hair. I have one brother and one sister, both older than me. My sister is the oldest and my brother is in the middle which leaves me as the baby. My mother loved to introduce me as the baby of the family, or as she likes to say it, 'He's my baby.' My mother had a miscarriage before I was born and so there's a 10-year age difference between my brother and me.

Even though my family lived in Corner Brook we spent a lot of time at my father's cabin which was located just past a provincial park called Big Falls Park. It was at the cabin where my father taught me how to fish, shoot and hunt. I was taught how to live off the land and also how to respect nature. At a very young age I could be found out in the middle of the woods catching rabbits and tracking animals. If I wasn't doing that I was out on the river with a fishing pole in my hand.

My parents let me take friends to the cabin with me. I guess they felt I might be lonely by myself. But I enjoyed being alone there. To me, there was something very special about the peacefulness. I remember being a small boy and loving to get up before everyone else and walking out to the Humber River to see if there were any moose out and about. Sometimes there would be loons out on the water. I loved to hear the loons call. I would sit on the same rock every morning and watch the water flow. Sometimes I would close my eyes just to listen to the sound of the water.

I have so many great memories from growing up at that cabin. One is of fires on the beach with Dad singing and playing guitar. Every night people from other cabins would get together for drinks or cards or whatever. It was about enjoying each other's company and helping each other if there was a job to be done. To me it was normal to want to help people because that was how I was raised. Helping people wasn't just what I wanted to do. It was all I knew how to do.

I still believe that one of the main reasons I joined the army was because of what my father taught me up at that cabin. All the things he taught me really helped me in my military career. By the time I was ready to join Dad had me skilled in shooting and surviving in the wilderness. I also wanted to help people who could not help themselves.

When I was in the second grade our house caught on fire. That night my sister stayed at her boyfriend's house, but everyone else was at home. Dad had a few drinks and was going to pass out on the couch. Mom talked him into going to bed and it was a good thing she did because that's where the fire began.

I remember being in the top bunk and Mom waking me and pulling me down as she told me to stay close to her because the house was on fire. Our house was a two-storey and we were standing in my bedroom. Dad told us to follow him downstairs where we would make our way out the back door. The back door was located next to the stairs so as soon as Dad hit the bottom he quickly opened the door. But once he did that there was a big explosion which drove Dad into the backyard and left us with no choice but to head back upstairs.

Now there was only Mom and my brother and I left in the house. Dad quickly recovered and jumped back on his feet. His worse fear had come true. His house was on fire and his family was trapped inside.

My brother led my mother and me back to my bedroom. He knew we had to jump so he grabbed Mom's sewing machine and threw it out the window. But as soon as he did the flames from the fire started to pour into the window. Without a second thought my brother grabbed the TV in my bedroom and threw it out the second window.

By this time I could not breathe because of the smoke that was filling the room. So I went back to my bed and covered my face with the blankets. At the same time my brother checked to see if it was safe to jump. Seeing that it was safe he told Mom to jump, and jump she did. The fall broke her leg but she was alive. Then he looked for me, but because of the smoke in the room he didn't see me. Since he couldn't see me he thought I had jumped when Mom did. Thinking that he was the last person left in the house he jumped. But once he got to the ground he soon realized that I was still inside.

I climbed out of my bed and walked over to the window. I could feel the heat from the fire on the floor. I looked out the window and saw people standing on our front lawn all screaming out to me. I looked back to see that the fire had worked its way up the stairs and was now just outside my bedroom door. I took a step back from the broken window and jumped through in a cannon ball shape. The only thing that didn't make it out alive was our cat. But if it wasn't for my brother's quick thinking neither Mom nor I would have made it out alive.

On my 17th birthday I joined the army reserves. I was a part of the Second Royal Newfoundland Regiment. It was there I learned to love the army life and I knew this was what I wanted to do for the rest of my life. I loved the way I felt when I put on the uniform and the way people looked at me. But I didn't just want to be a part of the army. I wanted to be the best. That's why wherever or whenever training was offered I jumped at the chance. I never turned down a course that was offered to me. In my mind I was only bettering myself. My training took me all over North America, spending as much time in the United States as I did in Canada. I was becoming a soldier.

But no matter where my training took me, I always came back to the cabin, the place I called home. The cabin was my happy place. During the years of training, whenever things became hard and I didn't know if I could go on, I would close my eyes and think about the cabin and once again find my center.

After eight years with the reserves I made the switch to the regular forces. I had to drop down in rank but I expected that. I dropped from a Master Corporal to a Private. I didn't want to leave the reserves but I wanted to be in the military full time so I knew I had to go.

I moved from infantry life to the life of a trucker. I became a Mobile Support Equipment Operator. My training took place in Borden, Ontario, and I found it was a fun course. I think the reason I enjoyed the course was because I was behind the wheel all the time. When I was in the infantry I had to walk or run everywhere with my gear on my back. But in the trucker world I drove and my gear was in the back or in the cab with me.

After my trucker training was complete I was posted to the 1st Service Battalion in Edmonton, Alberta, in 2004. When I first arrived I volunteered to help with weapons training but they just laughed at me because of my rank. But soon after I got there my file arrived and they soon found out what kind of training I had. Now that they knew about my infantry past I was used for all the infantry training. I was a Private, giving lectures to people with much higher rank than me. Sometimes it was even Generals.

In 2006, the build-up training for Afghanistan was going on in Edmonton, and with my infantry training and my trucker training I was an easy pick for the tour. I knew what I was going into by taking this tour and I didn't care. I wanted to fight for my country.

People ask me all the time, 'Why did you want to go there?' Here is my answer.

I did it because, well, imagine you are a baseball player and you spend years of your life training for a game. Don't you want to play at least one game to see if your training will work for you?

I wanted to know how I would act in battle, and I would find that out in Afghanistan.

My other reason is because the people I work with are like a family to me. My brothers-in-arms are with me when I eat, sleep, shower and bleed. They are the people who watch my back. I am the guy who watches their backs. So if my brothers are going into battle then I must go with them.

Afghanistan

Location: South Asia. North and west of Pakistan. East of Iran. Capital Kabul

Climate: Arid to semi-arid. Cold winters and hot summers. Population 29,928,987 (2005 est.)

Religions: Sunni Muslims 80 per cent; Shiite Muslims 19 per cent; Other 1 per cent

Among certain obligations of Muslims are to pray five times a day: at dawn, noon, afternoon, sunset and evening. Friday is the Muslim holy day and most shops and offices will be closed. Government offices and businesses may also close on Thursday, making the weekend Thursday and Friday. During the holy month of Ramadan all Muslims must fast from dawn to dusk and are only permitted to work six hours a day. (Info and map courtesy www.kwintessential.co.uk)

My Story

"Wake up man. Hey J. wake up! Come on, Jamie!"

I open my eyes slowly and see a guy standing at the foot of my bed in a uniform. My vision was blurred so I couldn't make out who it was at first. I shake out the cobwebs and focus on the face. It was Jeff Foley, my roommate.

Jamie – What are you doing here, man?

Jeff – The CSM (Company Sergeant Major) wants to see you.

I thought for a second, why did he want to see me? I just came off duty. Duty is when you have to spend the night at BN (battalion) building. It really sucks as a job. Duty is split throughout the BN, but in a fair way. You see, so many duties are given to each company, so if you're in a small Company (Coy), you can end up with a lot of duties.

But in saying that, you can also end up in a big Coy where you go for years without a duty. I got duties quite a bit but I knew guys who have been there for years and never got a duty. The only thing good about doing a duty was that you got to have the next day off. I just finished the duty so I had the rest of the day off. Why did I have to go back into work?

Jamie – Why does he want to see me?

Jeff – I don't know, man. I was just told to come and get you because you wouldn't answer the phone.

Well, that was true. No soldier answers the phone after work is done because they know you can always get called back to work. I don't think I know any soldier who does not have caller ID.

Jamie – Fine, man. Let me get dressed.

Jeff turns and walks out of my room, I listen to the sound of his boots walking on the kitchen floor. No doubt he is in the kitchen again. I grab some old clothes off my bedroom floor and put them on. I walk into the bathroom and splash some water on my face. I brush my teeth and give myself a long stare in the mirror.

So you can get a better picture of me. I'm six feet tall and about 220 pounds. I have a pretty big build but I am not one of these weight training monsters you sometimes see in the military. My size did not come from time spent in the gym but more because I am an outdoors kind of man.

I grew up at my father's cabin where I chopped wood, hunted, and did whatever I was told to do. I had a great childhood and was very close to my parents.

Jeff – You ready yet?

I snap out of it and run out to meet him in the porch. I put on my shoes and we both climb into his car.

My platoon lieutenant, Lt. Wilson, was at the front doors of the BN so I knew this must be important as he has never waited for anyone before. He walked up to me as soon as I entered the building and then as we went up three flights of stairs he talked to me.

The entire way up the lieutenant tells me a story of how CSM Bull called him today and asked him for his best man. He tells me how he could only think of one man and it was me. I have been around long enough to know when someone is blowing hot air up my ass. But I just play my role and thank him for the opportunity. I stand at attention at the CSM's door.

Jamie – You wanted to see me, CSM?

He looks up and just stares at me for three seconds, looking up at me with eyes that seem to look right through you. You just knew he was a little crazy, especially with that huge handlebar moustache. This moustache was a legend. Such a legend that tickets were sold each Christmas party to the winner who would get to shave it off.

CSM Bull was in his mid-50s with light brown hair that seemed to have a reddish tint. He was in great shape. Even though he was getting older it didn't stop him from keeping up with the young lads during PT. PT is our personal training, our time to get some exercise.

I entered his office and took a seat in the chair across from his desk. He spent the next ten minutes telling me about how the WO (Warrant Officer) called him today and asked him to send him his best man and how he thought of me.

Well, everyone keeps telling me how I am the best man for something but they won't tell me what. I think to myself, WO Baker is the PL WO (Platoon Warrant Officer) for the task force to Afghanistan. But as I think of it the CSM comes out and says it.

CSM Bull – We want you to join the task force to Afghanistan.

Jamie – Yes sir.

I didn't even have to think about it. A tour is what I have been waiting for. I have always wanted to do my job for real. For the years I have been wearing this uniform all I have been doing is training. But now I get to do it for real with real bullets. Plus I knew all the people on the tour. Heck, most of them were my drinking buddies.

The CSM smiled as he stood up and shook my hand then walked me to the door.

CSM Bull – Congrats Cpl. Young, the spot is yours. Remember, it was me who got you the spot.

Jamie – Yes sir, thank you, sir.

When I got outside, the lieutenant stopped me.

Lt. Wilson – Congrats on getting this tour, it's going to be one to remember. It was me that got you this spot, you know.

Jamie – Thanks sir.

I turn and walk away. I walk back down the three flights of stairs and headed for the cage where I knew the rest of the guys that I would be on tour with would be. The soldiers there were broken into four cages. There was Alpha, Bravo, and Charley and finally there were the guys going overseas. The cage was a place where all the platoon supplies were kept, and it was also used as a place for the boys to hang out. In the cage were Scott Parsons, Mike Jesso and Brian Brown. They were all just sitting back listening to the radio and talking.

Mike – Hey Jamie, what's going on, brother?

Jamie – I just got added to the tour.

Scott – No way. That's awesome. We were just talking about that. We heard Rogers was going to be added. Since he finished first of his QL5 (qualification level 5), CSM Bull was going to give him the spot.

Brian – But like I told the boys here, Rogers turned it down. Not too sure why, but he did.

Jamie – Hey, works for me.

Mike – Us too. We need good guys on this tour.

Brian –Yeah, I was talking to Sergeant Healey. He was talking about how dangerous this tour was going to be.

Scott – Whatever, man. I need the money.

We talked for about 30 minutes and then I decided to go back home. Foley was more than happy to drive me since it got him out of work for a few minutes.

Well, I'm going overseas too. Afghanistan. And this time we are not peacekeeping. A baseball player dreams about playing in the World Series, a hockey player dreams about winning the Stanley Cup, but a soldier dreams about war.

People watch TV, and they see the dangers of war and they think to themselves, 'How can these soldiers do that? Where do they find the courage to go and do what they do?' Well, I am going to tell you the reason. It's because we are family. They are my brothers and sisters and if they go to war then so shall I.

* * *

Afghanistan is a land-locked Asian country of 251,825 square miles (652,225 square kilometers) which is bordered by Pakistan, Iran, Turkmenistan, Uzbekistan, Tajikistan, and China. There are no reliable census figures but in 2005 the population was estimated to be 29,928,987. Afghanistan has historically been the link between Central Asia, the Middle East and the Indian sub-continent. The word Afghan has traditionally been used to designate members of an ethnic group also called the Pashtuns, but Afghanistan is a nation of many different nationalities as the result of numerous invasions and immigrations, and the whole of the population are now called Afghans. The official religion of Afghanistan is Islam. Followers of Islam are called Muslims. There are two main sects in Islam: Sunni (the largest) and Shiite. In Afghanistan 80 per cent of the population are Sunni Muslims and 19 per cent are Shiite Muslims.

* * *

Most Afghans are farmers. Largely subsistence crops include wheat and other grains, fruits and nuts. The opium poppy, grown mainly for the international drug trade, is the most important cash crop. Afghanistan is the world's third largest producer of opium and of hashish, obtained from hemp (cannabis). Opium, fruits and nuts, hand-woven carpets, wool, lambskins, cotton and gemstones are the country's main exports. As a result of years of war the export market has declined, except for the illegal trade in opium and hashish. Afghanistan has also become an important producer of heroin, which is derived from opium.

Most of Afghanistan is steep-sloped with mountains that range out from the towering Hindu Kush, the great mountain system of Central Asia. Hindu Kush is a 500 mile (800 kilometres) long mountain range that stretches between central Afghanistan and northern Pakistan. The highest point is Tirich Mir (25,289 feet or 7,708 metres) in Pakistan. The mountain range runs northeast to southwest across Afghanistan, dividing the country into three major regions: the *Central Highlands, the Southwest Plateau and the Northern Plains.*

The Central Highlands (160,000 square miles) form part of the Himalayas and account for roughly two-thirds of the country's area. This is an area of high mountains and steep narrow valleys which are historically important to the defense of the country. The most famous of these valleys contains the Khyber Pass, a strategic route to India. While summers are hot in the Central Highlands, the winters are very cold and many valleys are impassable. The *Southwest Plateau* (50,000 square miles) accounts for one quarter of the land and consists of high plateaus and sandy deserts. It is a largely desolate area crossed by several large rivers. The *Northern Plains* (40,000 square miles) is an area of fertile foothills and plains. The Amu Daria River runs through the edge of the foothills. This area is agriculturally important because of its rich soil and mild climate. The mineral resources of Afghanistan are mainly located in the *Northern Plains*. Afghanistan has significant deposits of coal, copper, gold, iron ore, lead, aluminum, natural gas, petroleum and precious and semi-precious stones which include emerald, lapis lazuli and ruby. It is estimated the country holds up to $3 trillion in untapped mineral deposits.

* * *

The problem is how do I tell Mom and Dad I am going to Aghanistan? I wonder if they have been watching the news and seeing what has been going on over there. Probably not, after all it's not on the news too much. I guess not enough soldiers have died yet. Stupid media. Nice to your face but a dick when you're not around. I am not taking anything away from cops, but when one of them dies it's all over the media. It's on every TV channel. But when a soldier dies it's like it's almost expected. I can hear someone saying, "You mean only five soldiers died on this tour, well that's not too bad." Maybe not too bad for you, but to me, that could be five friends of mine dead. No wait, let me rephrase that, that five brothers of mine are dead. And how about their families and loved ones? Do you think it was a good tour for them? Stupid media, I understand that they are only doing their job, but their job is messing up people's lives.

I snap out of these thoughts at the sound of the phone ringing. It was Mike. He told me he would be over to pick me up at nine and we were going out drinking. I figured it was a good idea. After all, after this weekend we head to Wainwright for two months to do our training.

I hang up the phone and look at my watch. 7:28. Nice. I've got lots of time to be ready for nine. I jump in the shower then get dressed. While I'm dressing, the phone rings. It's Vanessa. Should I answer it? I still have strong feeling for her and I think the world of her kid. But are they better off away from me? That way they don't have to go through the next seven months. Plus, what if I die over there? It's not right for them to have to go through that, especially not the kid. No, I won't answer it right now. I will call her tomorrow. I turn and continue to get ready.

* * *

That night, me and the boys go to a bar that we know oh too well. The bar is called 'Legends.' It's nothing special, just another dance bar. Most Army guys don't care for a dance bar but women do. So Army guys will go to dance bars to get drunk and try to pick up a lady friend for the night. But tonight it wasn't about picking up any women. It was just about the boys getting together for good times before the hard times begin.

At 2 a.m. the hunger pains start and we soon found ourselves outside the club looking for a place to eat. Scott spotted a Subway down the street so Mike and I decide to tag along with him. The rest of the boys have other ideas so we say our goodbyes and go our different ways.

Scott, Mike and me get our subs and sit and start eating. As I am chewing my food I look up and Scott has not taken a bite. He is just staring at a table where four guys were sitting. The guys were all laughing and joking about something. Scott soon heard what they were making fun of. Soldiers. And how it was stupid of them to go overseas.

You must understand, Scott does not take crap from anyone and is not afraid to confront someone about a matter such as this. Scott gets up and walks over to the table.

Mike – Oh no. Not tonight, Scott.

Jamie –Just let him go, Mike. Scott won't do anything, and even he is smart enough to know if he gets into trouble he is off the tour.

I said that to keep Mike calm because I knew that Scott was just crazy enough to fight those guys. I watched Scott walk over and stand next to one of the guys. The guy seemed a little on edge, almost as if he expected Scott to hit him. But Scott didn't, he just kept talking. The more Scott talked the calmer the guy got, and so did I. So the guy now feeling at ease decides to pick up his sub for a bite. That's when all hell broke loose. Turns out that was just what Scott was waiting for. As soon as the guy placed that sub in his mouth Scott hit him right in the mouth. I think his fist went straight through the sub before getting him in the face. There was an explosion of vegetables as the sub was blown apart. I jump from my seat and quickly grab Scott and head for the door with Mike close behind. Luck was with us. There was a cab sitting outside. We all jump inside and I give my address and we drive away.

I wake the next morning to the sound of the phone ringing. I check the caller ID. Vanessa. I've got to answer sometime, I guess.

Jamie – Hello.

Vanessa – Well, look who finally answers.

Jamie – Sorry, I was out drinking with the boys last night.

Vanessa – Oh, what's the occasion?

Jamie – We are going to Wainwright this Monday for two months. I found out yesterday I'm going to Afghanistan after Christmas.

Vanessa – You are? Oh wow.

Jamie – Yeah, so we were just out blowing off some steam and now I am paying the price.

Vanessa –Hangover?

Jamie –Big time.

Vanessa – Okay, call me when you feel better.

I hang up the phone and lie back on the bed. I know she still wants to be with me and I do really care for her. But I broke up with her because I knew that this tour was coming my way and I thought this would be best for all of us. It's bad enough that my parents will be worrying about me. I don't want to trouble Vanessa too.

I spend that whole day doing nothing, just being a vegetable on the couch watching TV. Sunday I packed my things for the field and that night Vanessa came over to watch a movie. Although we sat very close to each other all night there was no kiss goodnight. That was my plan to keep us just friends.

But for now it's bedtime for me. I've got an early rise for tomorrow I go to Wainwright. Wainwright, Alberta! Wow, what a place! It always confused me when we did training for the desert heat in the heart of an Alberta winter! But I guess if you train for one type of weather climate, you should be good to go in all types of weather climates!

When we hopped into our trucks for the long drive down the back roads to Wainwright it was early morning. The person I was supposed to have as a co-driver (someone to keep me awake, I'm assuming) took the bus instead. It was nice for a change not to have someone else aboard the truck with me. I'm not sure if I have a face that says, 'Tell me all your worldly problems or just tell me your whole life story!' This time, instead of hearing someone else talk, I had my iPod so I could listen to some tunes while I drove.

Once in the training area of Wainwright everyone was busy setting up tents. If you didn't look busy you were nabbed by the CSM to do some other company's job because they too were busy doing something else. I don't know how many times during that exercise I heard the words, 'Just grab a trucker! They're not doing anything!' If people knew how busy we were because we were always being tasked out to other companies they wouldn't say that.

The actual training for the tour didn't start until the halfway mark of our winter excursion. Weapons training, convoy training, DP (distribution point) training. You name it, we did it.

Some days in the field go by really fast and then there are those that go by so slowly you think they'll never end. We were out on the live fire range and doing 'Section Attacks' (which means teams of people moving forward under fire and providing covering fire), and of course this was one of those days that didn't want to end. It was raining and real cold! I'm not sure about you but there's something about holding a metal weapon in your hands when it's raining and cold that makes you colder. But as soldiers you suck it up and carry on.

I remember as a kid during the fall of the year I would do a lot of rabbit snaring. My dad taught me how to know which rabbit paths/buttons were the freshest and how to build a rabbit compound with multiple entrances. Of course if you built one you would have to cut alders and place them in the centre to help draw the rabbits in. Dad also taught me how to be humane when it came to killing them. It didn't seem to bother me one bit what type of weather it was when I was catching rabbits. I guess as a kid if you really enjoyed doing something you just did it and didn't worry about anything. So that's what I did on the range, I tried to put the weather out of my mind.

6 a.m. Time to get up. I sit up on my cam cot; my back is a little stiff from the comfort of the wonderful cam cot.

The army has been using these cots for years. I would love to see them buy us soldiers something better to sleep on. Something more comfortable. Rest is something everyone needs, even more so when you are a driver like me. As a driver in the military we are supposed to get eight hours of rest before driving. I have a feeling this rule will not be in effect in Afghanistan.

Sgt. Winchester – Time to get up, boys. Get washed up and get some breakfast.

I get up, toss my rifle over my shoulder, grab my shave bag and towel and head to the wash tent. While in the field we live in large tents, and one tent stays empty except for a few tables so people can wash and do whatever they have to do to get ready for the day. If you're wondering why I took my rifle, well, we train like we plan to live overseas. We don't go anywhere without our rifles.

A few of the boys and I head up to the kitchen trailer. The kitchen trailer is just a large kitchen on wheels. It's wrapped in a Mod tent. You enter on the right, get your food as you walk through the trailer and exit on the left. Then you walk over to the eating Mod. Yes, another tent filled with tables and benches where you eat your breakfast. There you would find juice, coffee, bread, fruit, and things like that. Once you finish breakfast you head back to your sleeping area and wait to find out what's going on for the day. Sergeant Winchester enters the tent.

Sgt. Winchester – Alright boys, grab full FFO and be on the road in 15. We're doing reflective shooting.

FFO means full fighting order: gun, vest, helmet, and eye wear. Everything you need for a fire fight.

We're going to have a day on the range. I like that. A lot of soldiers don't like shooting on the range. I don't know why. How you can join the army and not like to shoot doesn't seem right. Well, I know all the boys with transport and they like to shoot. I'm sure they think like I do, a day on the range is a day where you don't have to listen to any of the bullshit in the building where we work. We were going to be doing pair fire and movement. That's where one person shoots while another person runs. It's like practicing covering each other. All in all it was a good day. That night, we practice our night driving and driving with night vision glasses on.

Through the two months we spent in Wainwright we did some good training. We knew we would be driving through villages and Kandahar city in Afghanistan. So we built villages and practiced driving through these villages and what to do if we came under contact. What we would do if a suicide bomber hit us or maybe an IED (improvised explosive device), or even if there was a vehicle breakdown, something which was very possible since we were driving old trucks.

We spent a day at the gas hut. That was a great day because I watched one of the sergeants give us a ten-minute speech on how to put on the gas mask and how important this training was. Then once we got inside the gas hut he had trouble putting on his mask and had liquid coming out of every part of his face. I know it's not right to get pleasure out of someone else's misfortune but give me this one.

I remember Brian and his girlfriend at the time making fun of the sergeant later that night. Brian was lucky. His girlfriend was on the tour with him. I see a lot of married couples in the military that end up on opposite tours. People watch the news and see how soldiers are away from their loved ones for six to nine months. But how about the couples who are both in the military and who end up on opposite tours and see each other once in a year if they are lucky? Some soldiers spend years away from their families. I once met an American soldier who told me the last time he was home he bought a new truck. The truck is now paid for and he has yet to drive it because he is still away. How much would that suck? So many marriages don't make it because the husband and wife get so used to not having the other one around. Once you get used to being alone it's hard to live with someone. Must be hard on the kids too, but anyway....

* * *

The days turned into weeks and even though you did something different every day you still seemed to fall into some kind of routine. That's what the army is looking for and that's why we train so much. We practice things so much that after a while it becomes a part of you. It's like you can't help but do it.

10:00 p.m. and we are all given the evening off to relax. Everyone takes a nap first. After days of night driving it catches up with you. I decide to go out for a smoke. I push back the cloth Mod door and step out into the darkness. I look up at the stars; looks like there are a million of them. It makes me think back to Dad's cabin. That's the place I wish I was, Dad's cabin. It's nothing fancy, just a small cabin next to a river. A place where I don't have to get up on time for anything. Where I am not awakened by the sound of gunfire or a soldier telling me it's my turn on weapons watch. Oh, how I longed to sit next to the river and just listen to the water go by.

Just a few meters outside the tent was our smoking area. It was just a butt can with a few benches around it. As I walked over I saw soldiers all around the camp on cell phones. No doubt all saying good night to spouses and kids. I walked over and sat down. Over there was Adam Jones and Dan Harris. Dan was having a smoke while Adam spoke.

Adam – I'm serious, man. Well, at least that's the word right now.

Jamie – What's the word?

I pull out a smoke from a pack in the right breast-pocket of my combats as I sit down to join them.

Adam – I was just talking to Sergeant Healey. He was telling me how this is going to be the most dangerous tour Canada has seen since the war. Sarge thinks that a lot of us, if not all of us, will come back with a war story.

The war story, the one thing most soldiers look for. That one story they can tell other soldiers where they were in the shit, where their life was on the line. Every soldier wants that one close call, that one rush.

Jamie – Well, it's like we were told. This is no peace mission.

Adam – No man, not at all.

We spend about an hour that night just sitting there talking about what we might be facing when we hit the ground of the country they call Afghanistan.

6:00 a.m. And we are halfway through the second month of our training. Before we are out of our sleeping bags, Sergeant Winchester walks in.

Sgt. Winchester – Get up, boys. At 0900 we've got a General coming in to talk to us.

When a General comes that means we get to sit down and listen to him talk. A lot of soldiers look at that as a chance to relax. So we gather in the Mod tent where we eat. We all sit waiting for this man to walk in. He walks in and he is not alone; he has three officers with him. A man of that rank is never alone.

The General started to talk about Afghanistan and what we could expect when we hit the ground. He didn't beat around the bush, and we all respected him for that. He told us that our vehicles would be green, NOT TAN. He said that we would still be using the same vehicles we use in Canada but with the armour added. First thing I thought about was, if something is added it can fall off.

The General then spoke of our sleeping and washing quarters. After that, he spoke of the Taliban. He told us just how dangerous this mission would be and how we will all go down in history for this tour.

I have got to say, the man gives a good speech!

This General gets flown in by helicopter, gives us a 45-minute speech, and then leaves in a helicopter.

We spend the last two weeks of our time in Wainwright doing more driving. After all, that's what we will be doing in Afghanistan. It was now time to return to Edmonton and to Vanessa. She might not even want to talk to me. After all, I didn't call her the whole time I was out here training. I wanted to. My God, every night I wanted too. But I know I am doing the right thing. It's the right thing for Vanessa and Avery. They would only worry about me over there. I don't want to be a burden to anyone.

The whole drive back to Edmonton all I can think about is Vanessa and how much I want to see her. After two hours we are back at the BN. I can't believe I am actually happy to see the building after two months of living in a Mod tent. WO Baker tells everyone to leave everything just the way it is. Tells everyone to go home and get some rest and be back to work for 0800 tomorrow morning. I call Foley and he comes and picks me up and brings me home. When I get there I am surprised to see Vanessa sitting there waiting for me. She looked so beautiful.

Vanessa – Welcome home.

Jamie – Thanks, good to be home.

She walks over to me and hugs me. I hold her close and I can smell her shampoo. After months of smelling men her scent was like heaven to me. We sit down on the couch and she passes me a beer.

Jamie –Beer too?

Vanessa – I know you, Jamie.

That's true. She knew me better than anyone. We sat there for hours just talking. She wanted to know everything that I had been doing in Wainwright. It was nice to have someone to talk to who was not in the military, to get a point of view from someone outside the box. Later, we ordered a pizza and sat on the couch watching movies. She told me her son Avery was at his grandmother's and she could stay for the night.

The next morning when I woke up she was gone. All that was left was a note on the pillow saying, 'Call me later.' I jumped in the shower and then headed into work. We spend the morning unloading our trucks and washing our gear. The whole time we worked we talked about the hard times we went through during our training. We also talked about what to expect overseas. We talked about what each person was taking. Some guys were taking laptops; others were taking small DVD players. I wanted a laptop but I didn't have the money to spend on something like that. I have a portable DVD player so I will watch stuff off that.

In the afternoon we spent our time in the classroom learning about the different bugs over there. One that stuck in my mind was the Camel Spider. This was a spider that got its name because it was known to jump onto a camel and bite it. The venom from the spider bite would deaden the area and the spider would just start eating and the camel would not even feel it or know it was happening.

Well, you can just imagine the thoughts that went through our heads when the sergeant giving the lecture says, 'Why, the guts of the camel could fall right out and the camel wouldn't know until it's too late.'

Thanks for that image, Sergeant.

Almost everyone started to take quick glances at me and smile. They all knew how I felt about spiders. I hated them. I am not sure where my fear of spiders came from. Maybe one time when I was young my brother put a spider on me or something like that. Whatever the reason, it didn't matter now.

In the army, you try not to let the other soldiers know about something that bothers you. Soldiers are like college kids. They like to pick on each other. So I didn't want the people I worked with to know that I was scared of spiders because I knew I would have spiders thrown at me by my buddies.

I kept my fear of spiders quiet until one winter we were sent to Florida to do some training with the Americans. It was great how they picked the winter for us to go because the winter in Florida was like a summer in Canada. One night I was on watch or as some soldiers called it, 'fire picket.' When everyone goes to sleep someone has to be up watching the camp at all times. So guys would have to do one hour shifts throughout the night until it was time for everyone on the camp to wake up. The worst shift was always two to three or three to four in the morning. After my shift, I had to go to the bathroom. I had to do number two. The bathroom was a small brick building and once I was inside I saw what I would be using to do my business. The toilets were just one hole with a large board going across. The board had holes for people to sit on and do what they had to do.

While I sat there, my partner on the fire picket decided to use the bathroom as well. He walked in and sat a few holes over from me. He was only there a short time when he told me to look in the corner at the big spider. As soon as he said the word spider I snapped my head around and looked to where he was pointing. He wasn't lying, for there in the corner sat a huge spider. My body went cold when I saw the creature. My partner started to stomp his foot and every time he did the spider would inch its way closer to us. When I saw that I asked my partner not to stomp anymore. Hearing this, my partner decided to stomp his feet harder and more often. With that, the spider came at us with a speed that surprised us both. I took off running without pulling up my pants. I ran through the area where all the guys were sleeping with my pants down. After that night, everyone knew about my fear. I guess everyone in the classroom figured if a spider in America scared me then a spider in Afghanistan would be like torture to me. It's like I could see the pranks forming in their head as they grinned at me.

With the workday over I come back home and shower and get dressed. While I'm eating the phone rings. It's Vanessa, but I don't answer. I turn on the TV and keep eating. Just as I finish eating the phone rings again. This time it's Mike.

Jamie – Hello.

Mike – I will pick you up at 8. We're going out.

Jamie –We are?

Mike – Yes, after two months of training, we need to drink.

Jamie – I'll be ready.

He was right. We needed this. It was time to go blow off some steam. That night it was Scott, Mike, Brian, Dan, Adam, and me. We started at a small bar to prime ourselves and then we hit the dance bar. While we were there we watched as this guy slaps his woman. This is one thing that's not good to do in front of a soldier. A soldier sees a lot of things happen that they don't like and most times they can't do anything about it. So when they do see something they hate and there is something they can do about it chances are they will. As soon as Adam saw the slap he walked over and shoved the guy.

Adam – You don't ever hit a woman.

This guy did not waste any time. Right away he took a swing at Adam. Adam caught the guy's arm then wrapped his hand around the guy's throat. I watched as Adam choked the guy until he was lying on the ground on his back. He was about to pass out when Adam released him from his strong grip. The guy turned over and came too as Adam spoke.

Adam – Welcome back.

Then Adam punched him in the face, knocking the guy out. I watched Adam stand up in satisfaction and then I watched as the girl who just got slapped jumped on Adam's back and started to pull his hair and punch the back of his head. With that, we ran to his aid and we ended up all being kicked out of the bar. Bouncers never seem to care too much for us soldiers. I don't know why. Most soldiers like to drink so we bring in a lot of money. What's the problem? After that, though, we decided to call it a night.

The rest of the month of October was spent on the range. Shooting our C7 and also doing some 9mm shooting. A day at the range meant a day of betting. If you're a good shot it's a nice way to make a quick buck.

* * *

And then came the day I bought my plane ticket to Newfoundland for Christmas. One good thing about the military is that once a year they will fly you to visit your next of kin. If you're a single guy your next of kin is likely your parents. So that meant a free flight home for Christmas for me.

I could not wait for Christmas to see my old friends and family. Even though I lived in Edmonton, my heart and where I call home is Newfoundland. I looked forward to eating my mother's home-cooking, and Christmas is the time she is always baking cookies. When I was a kid, she used to make dozens of different kinds of cookies and when any of my friends would come over she would spend half the visit stuffing him with them. I guess that's just the Newfoundland way, if someone comes to visit you feed him or her.

I also remember Dad's friends coming over and the guitars coming out. Dad would spend half the night singing and playing his guitar. Everyone loved to hear Dad sing. I always wished I could sing but my father was the only one in the family who could sing.

November now, and our physical training was complete. The time for practicing driving, shooting and fighting was over. Now it was time to get our minds in the right frame of mind. The whole month of November was spent in a classroom learning how the Afghan people talked and behaved. We learned about their clothes and what they liked and what they hated. We wanted to know our enemy. One week was spent just trying to learn a few words in Afghan. We just wanted to know the basics like 'Stop or I'll shoot,' and 'Drop the gun.'

The government wanted us physically and mentally prepared. But half of us thought it was too much. It was okay for guys like me who lived in Edmonton but how about the guys that came from Nova Scotia? Guys who not only went overseas for six months but also spent six months before that in different province training for the tour.

The month of December quickly comes upon us and all everyone can think about is Christmas and how they can't wait for a little time off to spend with their families. I am the same as the rest of them. All I can think about is seeing Mom and Dad's smiling faces as I step off the plane.

We spend the days of December doing the paperwork that's necessary before we go. That includes writing a will. I just left everything to Mom and Dad.

Then it's our needles. I have never been overseas before so I have to get fourteen. But they can't give them all to me in one day so I get seven one day and seven another day.

They have us checked out by doctors. I like how they made us go through two months of training, and now if the doctor says no we can't go.

Next is our pay. They explain to us how we will be paid while over there and we choose how much we want going to one account and how much into another. Some people have money going to kids and different families.

On the final day of work before our Christmas leave the whole platoon is sitting on a set of bleachers waiting for someone to dismiss us. WO Baker walks out in front of the platoon and speaks.

WO Baker – You have all been asked to stand up and go into a mission where the enemy will be hard to recognize because he looks just like every other Afghan person. You have been asked to go over in the desert with green trucks and equipment. You have been asked to go on Canada's first tour in many years where it is not a peacekeeping mission. You have been asked to fight for your country.

And you have said yes. So now I ask something of all of you, go home, go to your families and hold them close, get drunk, sing songs, and have a very merry Christmas. Whether you tell them what you are going overseas to do I leave in your hands. For right now, the public is blind. But make no mistake, once our tour starts the people will know. But spend the time with them, and then come back ready to fight.

And with that we were dismissed for Christmas leave.

When I got back to my house it felt like I had just taken off a back pack. Like all this pressure was released. I think it was because I didn't have to worry about anything for the next three weeks. I could just relax and be me.

I had two days until I had to catch a flight to Newfoundland so I used those two days to pick up a few Christmas gifts. I got something for Vanessa and Avery, and Vanessa insisted I come over for an early Christmas dinner with them as I would be in Newfoundland during Christmas.

What a dinner she cooked. It was way too much food for the three of us but it was delicious. After dinner we opened gifts and I sat back and watched Avery open his gift. I could picture me sitting on the floor opening a Christmas gift and my father sitting right where I was, smiling as he watched me. Could I see myself being a father to this kid? I guess I could if watching him open his gift is bringing this much joy into my life. After the gifts, Avery picks out a movie and the three of us watch it. After the movie I say goodnight and go home.

The next morning, Dan comes to my house and brings me to the airport. I am very excited to be going home. Just wish I didn't have to spend the whole day flying. It's not that I am scared of flying. I just find it so boring. Just sitting there next to some stranger, and most of the time I end up sitting next to the old lady who smells like urine.

One time I was on a flight and I was in the window seat alone. We had a stopover in Toronto and it was at that time this old lady come on the plane and sat in the aisle seat in my row. So there was one seat separating me and her. By the look of her I could tell she was very nervous. She just sat in the seat tightly holding her purse and not saying anything to anyone. Suddenly, this white milky substance starts to drip from the compartment above us. She doesn't notice, but I do. So I say to her, 'I'm no plane expert but I don't think that is normal.' And I point at the substance.

Well, the old lady goes from sweet and innocent to evil and pissed off in a split second. She starts freaking out and pressing the button for the flight attendant to come. He tries to calm the woman down but she won't calm down. I am just sitting back loving it and wishing I had a camera because no one would believe me. In the end, she moved to another seat.

When I step off the plane I see Mom and Dad standing there. Mom opens her arms to me the same as she did when I was a small boy. I guess she still sees the little boy when she looks at me. I'm met with hugs and kisses from Mom and a handshake followed by a strong hug from Dad.

My father – Home again, eh?

My mother – Yes, he is, and for three weeks.

They both sounded so excited to see me and I felt the same about them. But all I could think about was how to tell them that their boy is going to go fight in the war. Mom and Dad always wanted me to join the army. My dad thought the army would look after me. They never expected me to go fight in a war. No Canadian ever expected us to be in a war in Afghanistan. But here we are and here I sit, trying to think of a way to break the news to them.

We get home and Dad turns on the TV to check the sports. Mom heads into the kitchen and turns on the kettle and then joins me and Dad in the living room.

Jamie – Have you been following what's going on in Afghanistan?

Father – A little, but not too much.

Mother – That's mostly Americans, isn't it?

Jamie – No. There are Canadians over there too.

Father – Can't be too bad. We haven't heard that much about it.

Maybe this is how I can play it off. I make it sound like it's not that bad a place. After all, my brother served over in Bosnia and he was okay.

Jamie – Yes, it's not that bad. If it was, the media would be all over it.

Father – That's right.

Mother – Why are you bringing this up?

Jamie – Cause I am going over there after Christmas.

They both stare at me for a few seconds without saying a word.

Father – You are?

Jamie – Yes, but don't worry. Like you said, it's not that bad. It will be just like Andy's tour.

I spend the next hour talking to my parents and trying to ease their mind about what their baby boy was about to go through. Even though I knew just what kind of danger I was going into I lied through my teeth, telling them that this was going to be more of an experience for me than anything dangerous. They seemed to take it well and believe me when I said it would not be that bad.

I wasn't home too long before a car pulled up in the driveway. The door bell rang and then the door opened. It was Jerry Walsh, one of my oldest friends. Jerry was a guy who lived for a party and someone I rarely saw upset.

Jerry – Knock, knock, knock. Merry Christmas. Is my boy home?

Mom laughs as I walk over to the top of the stairs.

Jerry – There he is. Welcome home, man.

Jamie – Thanks, man. Good to be home.

Jerry – Well, you have been home long enough. Now let's go. The boys are waiting.

That night, Jerry took me to the bar where I pretty much grew up. I spent many nights drinking with my friends in this old watering hole. I walked in to the sounds of cheers from my old drinking buddies. There was my cousin Billy, though he was more like a brother to me. There was Ricky Colman and Frank Towe. I could see them all standing at the bar with beers in their hands.

Billy was also holding a pack of darts. That meant it was to be drinking games with darts. Think of it kind of like the game horse with basketball. Everyone shoots and the person with the lowest score has to drink. We did that all night until Frank couldn't take anymore. Frank was not that good at darts so after a few hours he got pretty drunk, so drunk he started to fall asleep on his chair. Well, it wasn't too long before the bouncers noticed him sleeping in the chair. They come over and woke him up. His eyes shot open.

1st bouncer – Sir, we're going to have to ask you to leave.

Frank looks around, stands up.

Frank – Okay, I'll go. But I'm taking this stool with me.

The bouncers don't care, they let him go. I make sure Frank gets outside okay. After he walks through the door I go around to the side of the bar where there is a patio. When I look out I see Frank sitting on the stool and talking to people as they pass by. I stand there and watch him for a while. I wait until he is alone and then I call out to him.

Jamie – HEY FRANK!

Frank – YEAH?

Jamie – WHAT ARE YOU DOING?

Frank – I'M CHARGING PEOPLE COVER.

Frank was charging people as they came into the club. He was getting away with it because it was after 1 a.m. so there was no cover charge inside the club. Frank made $40 that night, enough for a cab ride home and a pizza. Well done, Frank.

I think almost every night I was home I was out somewhere with those guys. With those guys, the good times always seem to outweigh the bad. Funny, but they tell me that they hardly ever see each other. It's only when I'm around they all get together. I guess they would rather have no group then an in-complete group. I guess to them it just didn't feel right without all of us there.

Christmas Eve and the house is quiet except for the sound of the television. Dad is watching what he likes to call an 'action movie.' Mom is humming to herself while she knits another pair of socks for someone. She will watch an action movie but only with her ears. She doesn't like all the blood and dying so she turns to knitting instead.

I thought about going out with my friends tonight. Lord knows they've asked me often enough. But something about going out with them and leaving my parents home alone seemed wrong. This was Christmas Eve and at that moment the only people I wanted to see was the two who brought me into this world. They had no idea what their son was about to go do. If they had, they might never have let him leave their home again.

Christmas Day and I woke to the smell of a turkey cooking. No doubt Mom was up bright and early. Big dinner this year cause not only am I here but my sister Jackie and her husband Bob Baker will be here and their three girls: Jasmine, Janelle and Shania. If only my brother Todd and his wife and kids would come, that would be a perfect Christmas for Mom and Dad. All they ever wanted was to have their kids and grandkids close to them.

I come out into the living room and I see presents under the tree saying 'To Jamie from Santa.' Even though I am well into my twenties Mom still treats me like her little boy. I have to admit I kind of like it. We spent the morning opening gifts, drinking hot cocoa and talking about the good times spent together. Before we knew it was 11 a.m. and my sister and her whole crew were coming through the front door. Spending Christmas with my family was just what I was looking for in coming home. I know with these people no matter who I am or what I become they will stand behind me through it all.

I remember that as being one of my favourite Christmases. I don't know if it was because I knew I was going to a war. I don't know if it was because I didn't know if I was going to make it home. Maybe it was because the family spent more time with me because they knew where I was going. For whatever the reason, I am grateful for that time with them and it's a time I will always remember.

On Boxing Day, my brother Todd came to visit with his wife Carolann. Their kids could not make it. Mom had a ham prepared. Like there wasn't enough turkey to go around! But that's the way it is in Newfoundland. Ask anyone and they will tell you if you visit someone in Newfoundland around Christmas time one of two things will happen. Either you are going to get drunk or you will be fed. So Mom, knowing that her children were coming, had lots of food on hand and of course Dad had lots of beer on hand.

During the meal we talked about times at the cabin and about the Toronto Maple Leafs because that was our team. After the meal we watched a hockey game where the Leafs won.

Father to Mother – This has been one of the best days of my life. My team won and I got to sit and watch it with my two boys. What more could I ask for?

None of the boys in our family are big talkers except when we drink and then we have the biggest of mouths. Even though my brother and I were not much for talking to each other, before Todd left he took me aside for a chat. I could fool Mom and Dad about the dangers in Afghanistan but I could not fool him. He knew just what I would be facing over there and for the first time he was worried. I look back on that as a very special moment between brothers, perhaps like one that might have been shared between Walter and George McWhirter.

Well, three weeks sounds like a long time, but once it's over you look back and think to yourself where did the time go? Where did it go? My time in Newfoundland was up and it was time for me to head back to Edmonton. Time for this soldier to put his game face on and get ready to go face the desert sun of Afghanistan.

* * *

January. We are all back from leave. WO Baker gathers us all together to tell us how the flights to Afghanistan will work. He tells us how we will all be broken down into chalks and one chalk will be going over each week. (In military terminology a chalk is a specific aircraft load, especially a group of airborne soldiers that deploy from a single aircraft). Each chalk will have some people from each trade so we will all be broken into different chalks. Good news was each soldier gets the week off before their chalk leaves to be with their family. That sucked for me because my family was on the other side of the country.

When my chalk number was a week away all I did was hang out in my house and do nothing at all. When I was hungry I ordered food and then I just watched TV and played video games. The way I looked at it, just as well to be lazy now because after this week I would not have a chance to be lazy.

The day before I leave I have to come into the base for one thing. It's to get a pill we must all take while over there. The pill was to prevent malaria. You had the choice to take the once a week pill or the once a day pill. Each had its own side effects. I went with the once a week pill cause I figured I would never remember to take the pill every day. Most of the guys went with the same choice as me.

In that week I also spent some time with Vanessa. Every night with her was magical and I knew I loved her more than anything. But I could not bring myself to show her how I felt. Would what we have be able to withstand six months apart? And if we tried, would she break my heart and leave me halfway through my tour. I have seen that so many times, men getting notes from their soon to be ex-wives. I didn't want to be that guy. In my mind, even though I loved Vanessa, I didn't know if our love would be strong enough to stand this. So because of that, a big hug was exchanged and nothing more.

It's the night before I leave for Afghanistan. I am lying in bed. Can't sleep. My phone keeps ringing but I don't answer. I don't want to see anyone tonight. I just want to lie in my bed and get a good rest. I stare out my window at a street light. I watch a moth fly around the light. My thoughts are with Vanessa, my parents, and all the people I love. Am I ready for what may lie ahead? Time will tell. At least I know my family and Vanessa are behind me.

10 a.m. was the time we had to be at the base to catch a bus to the airport. Foley took me to the base even though I wanted it to be Vanessa. We stopped into Tim Horton's for a coffee. I thought one more before I leave the country. There was a rumour that a Tim's was going to be built on the camp overseas around April but we will see.

With coffee in hand we headed over to the base and met up with everyone leaving for Afghanistan. There was a huge crowd there, soldiers surrounded by loved ones. I saw tears rolling down the faces of some of the toughest men in the world, all because they will be away from their children for such a long time.

When they are away from their children for just a few days most parents cannot wait to see their smiling faces again. Imagine the soldier who leaves for six months or more. And how about couples who are parents in the military? The child goes six months without a mother, then six months without a father. It's quite the sacrifice.

At the airport, soldiers had their kit in a line-up. All kit must be checked before it's loaded on the plane. Each soldier had three pieces of kit. A barrack box, ruck sack, duffel bag. We had other barrack boxes sent over already. That stuff would meet us there. It was our UAB (unaccompanied baggage). I see Pat Layden. He and I were friends in the army reserves. That was the infantry days when I was younger and my knees didn't hurt so much.

Jamie – What's up, Pat?

Pat – Jamie, thank God you're here. Man, I don't know anyone here.

I look around the large gym floor and I recognize nobody.

Jamie – Me neither.

One thing I do notice when I look around the room and that was the media. They are always there with cameras going. They are all looking for the same thing, that perfect shot of a soldier crying with his kids. Or a crying child who hates to say goodbye to his/her mom or dad. I always thought farewells should be more of a private moment. Who really wants to watch soldiers and their families crying? There must be more important stuff going on? I really wanted to go ask the media that. But if I did I would most likely get into trouble.

The bag checkers come out and set up their tables. There are four of them standing there with their white gloves on. Four at a time the soldiers walk up to the tables with all three pieces of their kit and place them on the table that separated them from the bag checkers. Each bag, if locked, was unlocked by the soldier. The bag checkers were checking for things like large knives, booze, lighters, etc. After the bags were checked and loaded into a big truck we got aboard a bus that sat outside the building. The bus was full of soldiers all listening to their own MP3 players, and I was about to do the same. I figure I can catch a quick nap on the way to work. My old infantry master warrant officer always said a good soldier sleeps when he can.

* * *

Ahmed Shah, a Pashtun, became the ruler of Afghanistan in 1747, and his Pashtun clan was to rule the country in one form or another for the next 200 years. Ahmed Shah was able to unify the different Afghan tribes and went on to conquer considerable parts of what are today Iran, Pakistan, northern India and Uzbekistan. However, his successors were unable to hold his vast empire together and within half a century much of it was seized by rival regional powers within the country. Rivalry for the throne led to many bloody civil wars.

Beginning in the 1800s, Britain and Russia began vying for Afghanistan. Britain was able to retain control of Afghanistan until 1919 when the country declared its independence. Britain conceded independence but the subsequent outbreak of civil war forced Amanullah Khan, the reigning king of Afghanistan, to abdicate in 1929. Mohammad Nadir Shah, who had been exiled to France following the 1919 Afghan War, then returned to Kabul and seized the throne. When he was assassinated four years later, his son Zahir Khan succeeded him and ruled for forty years. In 1973, while Zahar Khan was in Italy undergoing eye surgery, his cousin and former Prime Minister Mohammed Daoud Khan staged a coup which resulted in the ousting of the king and the establishment of a republic.

Daoud proclaimed himself president of the new republic with help from the People's Democratic Party of Afghanistan (PDPA), a pro-Moscow Communist party. In 1978, the PDPA, led by Nur Mohammed Taraki, Babrak Kamal and Amin Taba, seized power from Daoud in a military coup. Daoud and his family were killed and Taraki took power as head of the country's first Marxist government. In March 1979, Hafizollah Amin became prime minister. On September 14, Amin overthrew Taraki, who was killed.

* * *

The PDPA moved to replace religious and traditional laws with secular and Marxist-Leninist ones. Equality of the sexes was declared and women were guaranteed equal education and job security. Women were given the right to vote and forced marriages were banned. At the same time the PDPA was acting progressively in its treatment of women, it imprisoned, tortured or murdered thousands of the traditional elite, the religious establishment, and the intelligentsia. The secular nature of the PDPA and its heavy dependence on the Soviet Union made it unpopular with the majority of the Afghan population. Most of the new government's policies clashed directly with the traditional Afghan understanding of Islam.

In 1979, the Soviet Union invaded Afghanistan with the approval of the PDPA. Amin was killed and Babrak Karmal became president of Afghanistan. Islamic fundamentalist groups immediately began waging guerilla warfare against the Soviets. The mujahedeen, as the Islamic guerillas were called, were helped by the American CIA, which provided billions of dollars worth of weapons to help destroy Soviet tanks and airplanes. The mujahedeen were trained in Pakistani camps with US support.

* * *

In 1989, the Soviets withdrew from Afghanistan after a fruitless ten-year struggle that killed as many as 60,000 of their soldiers and cost an estimated $20 billion. The Soviet occupation resulted in the deaths of up to two million Afghans, mostly civilians. About six million Afghan refugees subsequently fled to Pakistan and Iran, with 38,000 making it to the United States and more to various parts of Europe.

After withdrawing from Afghanistan, the Soviets continued to provide military assistance worth billions of dollars to the PDPA. This assistance continued up until the collapse of the USSR in 1991.

Mujahedeen fighters toppled what was left of the PDPA government in 1992. Eventually the seven main parties allied into a political block called Islamic Unity of Afghanistan Mujahedeen. Muslims from other countries assisted the various mujahedeen groups, which were all Sunni Muslims, with the majority being Pashtun. The rule of the mujahedeen soon disintegrated into civil war. The period from 1992-1994 saw the disintegration of the coalition and the formation of the Islamist Taliban movement in Kandahar.

* * *

Osama bin Laden, who was originally from a wealthy Saudi Arabian family, first went to Afghanistan in the 1980s in order to help finance, recruit and train Soviet-fighting mujahedeen. He became a prominent organizer and financier of an all Arab Islamist group of foreign volunteers. His Maktal-al-Khadamat, the forerunner of al-Qaeda, funnelled money, arms and Muslim fighters from all around the Muslim world into Afghanistan with the support of the Saudi and Pakistani governments.

The Taliban emerged in northern Pakistan in the early 1990s following the withdrawal of Soviet troops from Afghanistan. A predominantly Pashtun movement, the Taliban came to prominence in Afghanistan in the fall of 1994. The Taliban promise in Pashtun areas of Pakistan and Afghanistan was to restore peace and security and enforce their version of Sharia or Islamic law once they were in power. The Taliban supported public executions of convicted murderers and adulterers and amputations for those found guilty of theft. The Taliban banned television, movies and cinema and disapproved of girls ten and over going to school. Women were forbidden to work outside the home, to seek help from a male physician or even to leave their homes unless accompanied by a male relative. Men were required to grow beards and women to wear the all covering burka.

The Taliban were initially welcomed by war weary Afghans. Taliban popularity was largely due to their success in stamping out corruption, curbing lawlessness and making roads and areas under their control safe for commerce to thrive.

* * *

In 1996, with the Taliban in power, bin Laden established his al-Qaeda base in Afghanistan and declared war against America. His role in a 1998 series of bombings of US embassy buildings which killed and wounded hundreds of people landed him on the FBI's most wanted list and led to the US launching a missile strike at suspected bases of his in Afghanistan. In 1999, the United Nations imposed an air embargo and financial sanctions in an effort to get Afghanistan to hand over bin Laden.

In 1996, with the help of backing from Pakistan and al-Qaeda, the Taliban controlled 90 per cent of Afghanistan. They'd captured Kabul after overthrowing the regime of President Rabbani and moved their capital from Kabul, centre of the nation's wealth and foreign embassies, to the much poorer city of Kandahar. In 1997, the Taliban were recognized as the legitimate rulers of Afghanistan by Pakistan and Saudi Arabia.

In March 2001, when the Taliban were at the height of their power, they drew international condemnation when they began destroying statues across the country, including the two Bamiyan Buddhas which had been carved into a sandstone cliff near Kabul almost 2,000 years earlier. The larger male Buddha towered almost 170 feet and was the world's tallest standing Buddha, while the smaller female Buddha stood 114 feet. The Taliban ordered the Buddha destruction as part of its campaign to destroy pre-Islamic artifacts which were considered an assault on Islam.

According to a United Nations report, the Taliban carried out systemic massacres of civilians while trying to consolidate their control over northern and western Afghanistan. Fifteen massacres were reported between 1996 and 2002. In one instance, 4,000 civilians were executed and many more were tortured. The UN documents show evidence of Arab and Pakistani support troops involved in these killings. People in many Afghan villages reported seeing Arab fighters carrying long knives which were used for slitting throats and skinning people.

In areas of Afghanistan that were controlled by the Northern Alliance, which was led by Ahmad Shah Massoud, an opponent of both the Soviet occupation of Afghanistan and the Taliban, there were no reports of human rights violations. As well, democratic institutions were set up and a Women's Rights Declaration was signed. In the post-communist Islamic State of Afghanistan, the man called the Lion of Panjshir (Massoud was born in the town of Bazarak in the Panjshir Valley in northern Afghanistan) had served as minister of defense. Following the rise of the Taliban in 1996, he returned to the armed opposition and served as military and political leader of the Afghan Northern Alliance, also known as the United Islamic Front for the Salvation of Afghanistan.

* * *

In August 2001 the American government agreed on a plan to give support to the anti-Taliban forces of Massoud who wanted to create a democratic form of government in Afghanistan. But Massoud was assassinated on September 9, 2001, likely at the instigation of al-Qaeda.

First came Massoud's death and then came the horrific events of 9/11.

At 8:45 a.m. on Tuesday, September 11, 2001, nineteen militants associated with al-Qaeda hijacked four airlines and carried out suicide attacks against targets in the US. Two planes were flown into the North and South Towers of the World Trade Center in New York City (both towers collapsed within two hours), a third plane hit the Pentagon just outside Washington, and a fourth plane crashed into a field in Pennsylvania. More than 3,000 people were killed during the attacks, 246 people on the four planes (there were no survivors), 2,606 in the World Trade Towers, 125 at the Pentagon and more than 300 firefighters. The 19 hijackers were also killed.

* * *

After 9/11, American President George W. Bush demanded the Taliban turn over bin Laden and al-Qaeda leaders operating in Afghanistan or face attack. The Taliban asked for proof of bin Laden and al-Qaeda involvement in the attacks on the States. The States refused to provide evidence.

On October 7, 2001, armed forces of the United States, the United Kingdom, France, and Australia along with the Afghan Northern Alliance officially launched what was called Operation Enduring Freedom in order to oust the Taliban regime. The invasion began with American and British forces conducting air strikes. Within two months the Taliban had been removed from office, but the war continued as US and coalition forces attempted to defeat a Taliban insurgency campaign based in neighbouring Pakistan.

In December 2001, Hamid Karzai, a member of the Northern Alliance, was chosen as head of the Afghan interim administration. In 2004, Karzai became the first democratically elected president of the Islamic Republic of Afghanistan. In the past decade there have been many attempts to assassinate Karzai by groups associated with the Taliban and al-Qaeda.

* * *

From 2001-2011, Osama bin Laden was a major target of America's so called War on Terror with a $25 million bounty on his head. Just a few months after the 9/11 attacks on the US he was believed to be cornered in Tora Bora, a cave complex in the Hindu Kush mountains in Afghanistan, but the December mission aimed at killing or capturing him failed and he was able to escape to Pakistan where he began rebuilding his organization.

In August 2003, in its first mission beyond Europe's frontiers in its 54-year history, the North Atlantic Treaty Organization (NATO) took formal control of an Afghan multinational peacekeeping force. In 2008, more than 200 American and NATO troops were killed in Afghanistan. Civilian deaths in attacks by US and international forces were also rising as Afghans protested the presence of foreign troops in their country.

In 2004, bin Laden finally claimed responsibility for the 9/11 attacks on the US, citing American support of Israel, the presence of American troops in Saudi Arabia and sanctions against Iraq as his motives. He remained at large until May 2, 2011, when he was shot and killed in a private residential compound in Abbottabad, Pakistan, by an American Navy SEAL commando team in a covert operation ordered by American President Barack Obama.

* * *

In February 2009, President Obama said he would send 17,000 more American troops to Afghanistan. In December 2009 he promised to send another 30,000 troops. In June 2011, a month after the death of bin Laden, Obama said American goals in Afghanistan had largely been realized and the plan was to get US troops out of the country by 2014.

In August 2012, the US military reported 2,000 dead in Afghanistan. The following month, the US completed withdrawal of 33,000 troops who had been deployed in the 2009 surge. Another 86,000 troops remained in Afghanistan.

* * *

Canadians first learned their soldiers were members of a top secret commando group in Afghanistan on December 19, 2001. But it wasn't until February 2002 that the first battle group from the Princess Patricia's Canadian Light Infantry (PPCLI) arrived in Kandahar on a six month mission to assist with American-led Operation Enduring Freedom. In April, four members of the PPCLI were killed and eight others injured when they were attacked by a US pilot in a friendly-fire incident. The Canadians were back home by the end of July.

From August 2003 to December 2005, Canadian troops were based in Kabul as part of a NATO-led International Security Assistance Force (ISAF), which was attempting to stabilize Afghanistan and neutralize the Taliban and al-Qaeda. On July 31, 2006, NATO troops took command of all military operations in southern Afghanistan. ISAF had troops in Kabul and the north and west of the country. For six months ending on November 1, 2006, Canada also held command of a Multinational Brigade for Southern Command. During this period, Operation Medusa, a major offensive against insurgents in Kandahar province, was launched.

* * *

The flight over to Kabul was very long. I felt as though I was sitting in the back seat of my father's car back when I was a kid and the trip felt so long and you just wanted it to be over.

The doors of the plane open. I watch as the orange light of the setting sun hits the face of the flight attendant. She squints as the light hits her eyes. I rise from my seat and stand in line as we slowly exit the plane. I step out onto the stair ramp. The first thing I notice is the wind. But it wasn't like the wind I knew well from Edmonton. This wind was warm, really warm. I took a second and gave a quick look around. The ground was flat and sandy. I could see some small buildings and some Mod tents set up. (Army tents with a frame, windows and doors are called MOD. As in modular). To me it didn't feel like war here.

It seemed like just another exercise. It seemed like a nice place to do a tour.

Here in Kabul is where we were issued our weapons and our ammo. This is where we found our vests and our helmet. But to me it still felt like an exercise. When we were given our ammo I looked down and watched the bullets go into my magazine (mag) just like I have done so many times before. But this time the bullets were real, they were not just blanks. The only time I have ever loaded real bullets into my C7 was to shoot on the range. But we were nowhere near a range. I had five mags loaded, four on my vest and one on my weapon. I also had extra ammo in a pouch attached to my vest. It was up to you how much you wanted to carry. I carried enough to load all my mags again and so ten mags in total. Each mag had 30 rounds. Also in my vest was first-aid equipment, gun oil, and sunscreen, everything I thought I might need in the desert.

Once we all had our gear, we set it down in rows of three and were told to go get supper from the mess. One thing I can say about the mess halls in the Canadian army is that they are usually pretty good and the one in Kabul was one of the best. Fresh fruit, ice cream bar, and the cooks really knew what they were doing.

I have always been a big fan of yogurt and when I saw the yogurt there I knew I had to try it. Well, I tried it and it was the best yogurt I have ever had in my life. I started bringing it to my friends, telling them they had to try it. I really wish they had this yogurt in Canada.

Once our bellies were full it was back to our gear. We were told to put on our gear and get ready because the Herk (Lockheed C-130 Hercules aircraft) was ready for us. One by one we loaded into the huge plane and did our best to get comfortable for the flight from Kabul to Kandahar.

As the Herk came in close for a landing the plane had to swing left and right just in case a Taliban soldier wanted to take a pop shot at a plane landing, just for fun. We land and the engines are shut off. It takes a few minutes for the crew to open the door of the plane. With the engines shut off and the air conditioning not going it doesn't take long before the temperature in the plane starts to rise. Sweat starts to form on my head and run down my face. I look around and I see that I am not the only one with sweat rolling down their face. Everyone begins to look around wondering what is going on? And what is taking so long?

Finally the door opens and we are greeted by sand blowing into the plane and sticking to our sweaty faces. 'Welcome to Afghanistan, Jamie,' I think to myself.

One by one we step out of the plane. As soon as I step out the sun hits me and the reality of it all sinks in. I am no longer in Canada. No place in Canada is this hot, especially not in February.

We follow in line around the plane to what looks to be an old hangar. It was made of wood with every window smashed out. On the ceiling inside birds had made their nests. I didn't go inside to look around.

We are greeted by WO Baker and a Major, whose job it was to give the speech and the tour of the base to the new people coming in. John Butler was there in a HLVW (a heavy logistics vehicle wheeled, also known as a heavy utility truck). John's job was to transport our kit bags from the plane to where we would be sleeping. I go over and say hi to John and he tells me about how busy they are. Then we are told to load into the bus. I tap fists with John and jump onto the bus.

We go see the PX (post exchange). The PX was like a general store where a soldier could get little things he/she needed. Once the tour was over we were dropped off at Canada House. This was where soldiers could get a pop, smokes, and junk food or even rent movies. Plus there was a satellite TV, a place for us to watch the NHL playoffs. Also on the camp site were a Burger King, a Pizza Hut and a Subway. They were still building the Tim Horton's.

I go to my Mod tent. I find my name on the wall and see where I am, third room on the left. Each room is separated by blue tarps. It wasn't the best of rooms but it was better than one room shared by everyone. Inside my little room was a cot with a mattress on top of it. Scott burst into my room carrying a long wooden board.

Scott – Here, man. Put this under your mattress, it's more comfortable.

Nice. I had Scott in the room next to me. On the other side was Jason Morgan. Two guys who were always good for a laugh. I set up my bunk and make spaces for each thing I owned. I tried to make my room my own.

Once we are all settled away I come outside. As luck would have it, it was the same time the boys were off for the day. Some of the boys were out on convoys. Most infantry units had one trucker with them. The trucker would drive an HLVW with things like rations or water, or whatever the infantry needed.

Our Mod tents for sleeping were the half-moon shaped ones. They were all in rows. When you stepped out of your tent the first thing you saw was the door of another tent. Some tents had a concrete square outside the door. Some soldiers took it upon themselves to build nice looking patios in front of their tent. I remember some people had picnic tables. I guess you make the most out of what you have.

There were tents where all the truckers slept. My tent had the concrete block, and another tent had a fridge outside. We kept the fridge full of bottled water. One tent had a patio and we all shared the picnic table that was there. The table was where we sat to tell stories of what had happened that day. If someone had been on a convoy it would be their turn to tell the tale of the good points and the bad points. It was like we were learning from each story that was told. We'd spend the rest of the night telling stories and smoking.

The first morning I awoke and tried to start a morning routine. I brushed my teeth, washed my face, that sort of deal. But it's something different to be carrying a rifle when you are trying to get ready for your day. After I cleaned up I headed for breakfast with a few of the boys. It's time to try the food I will be eating for the next few months. I have to say it's not bad.

After breakfast, I head up to work. Our compound was a dirt parking lot surrounded by a wire fence. Everything parked in there was either a green army truck or what we called a jingle truck. A jingle truck was a small bus or a civilian sized truck that we'd borrowed from an Afghan. We called them jingle trucks because the Afghans liked to cover their vehicles with colourful ribbons and little bells that jingled and shone. Very 1970s retro stuff.

After about an hour of being at the compound we get the word that one of our convoys has been hit by a suicide bomber.

Jamie – Who was in the convoy?

WO – Let's see, Sergeant Winchester is there, Harris is there, Wallace and Johnson.

Everyone in the convoy was a good friend of mine. We sit and wait for some new news or to see the guys come back into the compound. Millions of different thoughts rushing through our heads, the not knowing if your friends are alive or dead was difficult for me. Finally, vehicles come back into the compound. All the boys are there except for Harris. We greet the boys with water and a place to sit to relax.

Jamie – Where is Harris?

Sgt. Winchester – He went down with the wounded. Don't worry, he is okay. He was just helping get everyone to the hospital.

We all listened to the sergeant tell the story of what happened. He told us it was not just a suicide bomber. The bomber was driving a vehicle and he had six rounds of artillery ammo on board when it detonated besides the LAV (light armoured vehicle). The sergeant could see that one of the crew members was badly hurt. His arm was almost completely severed. The sergeant, knowing that this guy's life was on the line, had Wallace drive the Bison (an armoured personnel carrier) up to the LAV to help. Once they were there, Wallace dropped the back door of the Bison and the soldiers started to exit the LAV and get aboard the Bison. Soldiers in the LAV did first-aid on the injured crew member. They all got inside the Bison and Harris did his best to hold the injured guy down and keep him from moving around.

With everyone loaded in the Bison they started back to the camp. Wallace knew that the injured soldier didn't have much time so he pushed the Bison as hard as he could. He pushed it so hard that the engine burst into flames just a few meters short of the main gate.

With the vehicle in flames, smoke begun to fill the inside of the Bison. Wallace tried to open the back door but it was jammed and wouldn't open. The passengers inside were trapped. The top hatch, or as we call it the family hatch, was pried open manually and the injured soldier was passed up through the hatch and on to the top of an LUVW (light utility vehicle wheeled) that had been pulled up to the burning Bison. Harris then crawled on top of the LUVW to hold the injured soldier down. Once they were both up there, Harris gave the 'good to go' thumbs up and off they went to the hospital.

The sergeant continued to tell us that he then turned his attention to the driver. When he looked he saw that Wallace was suffering badly as a result of the heat from the engine fire. With one quick moment, the sergeant grabbed Wallace by the back and pulled him out of the fire.

I listened to the story the sergeant told. I have been here for one day and already one of our convoys has been hit. I guess there is no such thing as warming up to the job.

After the sergeant finished talking I headed down to the hospital to check on Harris. When I got there he was not hard to find. He was sitting outside the hospital smoking. I pulled up in one of those jingle trucks and he quickly jumps up and gets in.

Jamie – How ya doin, man?

Harris – I'm okay, man. Just a little shaky.

Jamie – Well, I think you have every right to be.

I listen as Harris gives me his side of what happened. The whole time he's talking he stares down. Because I am driving I cannot tell what he is staring at or if he is even staring at anything at all. He talked about how he can still hear that guy screaming and how he watched the guy's face go from reddish colour to pale white. Harris closed his eyes and took a long puff of smoke.

Harris – The things we do to pay the bills, eh Jamie, my boy?

We both have a laugh and head back to our sleeping Mods. That night we all gathered around the picnic table and listened to each person talk about what happened that day. We all wanted to hear every detail and to learn from it. While we talked, other Canadians from different bases came to say hello and they were glad the boys were okay.

Sure, in the military the army makes fun of the air force and the air force makes fun of the navy and we all give each other a hard time. But when we were in Afghanistan it didn't matter what trade you were, it didn't matter what country you came from and it sure didn't matter what colour your skin was. Here it wasn't about race, it was about life and all our lives were about to change here. We were all in this together, like one big family. If one person dies we all feel the pain. It doesn't matter where the person is from.

Even though we had a convoy hit and people were hurt we still called it a good day. After all, nobody died. In Afghanistan, and in our line of work, if you have a bad day it means someone died. It was getting close to 9 p.m. when Harris asked me if I was hungry.

Jamie – Burger King?

We both agree a burger would go down good. We grab our rifles, sling them over our shoulders, and head up towards Burger King. I can tell Harris was shook up over what happened today. We didn't say much the whole way up to the burger joint. Not even when we ordered our burgers. I thought to myself that if he felt like talking I would let him start. I didn't want to bring it up if he didn't feel ready to talk. We got our burgers and walked back down to our tent area. By now the picnic table was empty. All the boys were either in their bunks or in the shower. We sat in silence and ate our burgers. When we were finished I tossed him a smoke. The smoke must have been the key because Harris finally started to talk to me. He told me about how he could still hear the screaming. The images of what happened today were not the problem for him. It was the sounds and how he kept hearing them over and over in his head. Not much you can do to comfort a man in a time like this. Best thing you can do is listen and so that's what I did.

* * *

It's 6 a.m. Another day. I eat my breakfast and hitch a ride to work. Since we are transport we have one perk and that is we always have a vehicle to get us to and from work. Once at work, the people who have taskings (specific jobs) such as camp refueling or other camp duties where transport was needed would head out to those taskings. Other taskings could be driving a bus and transporting people around the camp, moving large C containers around with our sixteen ton truck, or even picking up the luggage of incoming soldiers. These were the camp duties for transport and we also had to do other jobs such as gate duty, which is pretty much guarding the front gate of the camp. Or some of us worked the market. The market every Sunday was pretty much like a giant garage sale for the Afghan people. It was a chance for them to set up a store so us soldiers could walk through it and buy what we liked. That was where we bought our smokes. At three bucks a carton you could not lose. They also had things like movies at very cheap prices, countless boxes of jewellery. Whatever you could think of they had.

People who didn't really have anywhere to be right away or their tasking didn't start till later in the day hung around in the transportation office. There were two offices in the compound where we worked. One was where our Officer, Lt. Travis, worked along with our dispatcher. We called him Doc because his last name was Holiday. WO Baker was in there too. The other office was where the sergeants had a desk and the corporals and privates hung out. There were a few computers there so people could check their military email or even check out a few websites or maybe their bank account. We called this office the driver's room.

Also on the compound was a large Mod tent we had set up as our stores tent. In this tent you could find the tools we needed to check out our vehicles before a convoy. It also had fridges, one full of bottled water, the other full of different flavours of Cola and also some Red Bull.

I was only in the driver's room a short time when the WO told me I would be going on the range to zero my weapon. This is good news to me because I do love shooting my C7 rifle. But I wasn't the only one shooting today. There were a few of us. We all loaded onto one of the small buses and headed out to the range on the camp. On the range we would shoot five rounds and then check the grouping. Grouping means how close together the holes in the target were. After a few groups of five my rifle was sighted in. As each of us sighted our rifles we jumped back on the bus. Once we had all finished we headed back to the compound.

I spent the rest of the day checking out the condition of the vehicles we would be using while on this tour. The trucks were not in too bad shape. As far as an HLVW goes, they are in good shape. That's pretty much thanks to the maintainers in the Canadian Forces. Maintainer is army talk for mechanic and we have some of the best here in Canada. Something tells me those boys are going to be busy during this tour.

On the top of the truck was a large air conditioner. That is something that was needed. We were told we could get brain damage if we tried to drive without it turned on because it would get that hot inside the truck. I sat inside the truck and closed the door. I placed my hands on the wheel and peered out the small part of the windshield where I would be looking when I drive. It was a thick piece of bullet-proof glass and with the door closed it sure was dark. I wonder how this will affect my night vision glasses (NVGs). The NVGs need some light to work and inside the truck there wasn't much.

I climbed out of the truck and walked over to the stores tent where I grabbed a bottle of water out of the fridge. I placed the bottle of water on the table and then I pulled out my pack of smokes and lit one. When I came back to my bottle of water I was surprised to see it looked frozen. Was I freaking out? I was sure the bottle of water was not frozen when I grabbed it. I walked over to the fridge and again I pulled a bottle of water. This time I made sure that it wasn't frozen, that it was just water. I placed the bottle on the table and sure enough it started to freeze from the bottom up. It was so cool to watch it freeze right before my eyes. It reminded me of a TV show I once saw that played nature through time. It showed trees and flowers growing.

WO Baker has us all gather in the driver's room to talk to us. His speech is about our rules of engagement cards and how important they are and that we have to keep them on us wherever we go. The cards have all our rules for over here. It tells us stuff like how we can't shoot at anyone until we are shot at. We can only use the minimum force needed for us to be safe. It means, and I asked to be sure, if me and a friend are out somewhere and an Afghan walks up and shoots my friend in the head and kills him and then drops his gun I can't do anything.

Jamie – If someone shoots my buddy, he's a dead man.

The men who stood there with me all agreed with my statement.

5 p.m. For the guys around the compound, it was quitting time. Doc comes out with what's going on tomorrow. I get camp refueling with Brad Richards.

Brad was a great worker and one hell of a drinker. I remember when I first got posted to the BN, Brad and I were in the same platoon. At the time he was the stores man for the platoon which means he took care of the equipment the platoon used. Well, Brad was the arm wrestling champ and we hung out in the cage where the equipment was. In the cage Brad had a huge bench set up which made the cage look like somewhat like a store. You walked into the cage and asked Brad for something and he would walk out and place it on the counter. But as the arm wrestling champ he also loved to put his arm on the counter and take someone down. It was funny to me because when you looked at him he didn't look like some big guy who went to the gym all the time. He was just a big strong guy.

Tomorrow sounded like a good day to me. When we all found out what we were doing we jumped on one of the jingle buses and headed for the sleeping area. Once in the sleeping area, some of us went to eat, like I did, and others showered, changed clothes, or called home. I found it nice to sit and enjoy a meal in the air conditioned area. Plus it was cool to see soldiers from different countries and see what kinds of personal weapons they had and what their uniforms looked like.

After my belly was full I headed to my room and got changed into shorts and a T-shirt. Grabbing my smokes and my rifle, I set out for the picnic table. There were already guys sitting at the table when I get there. The boys are talking about how the PX has folding lawn chairs for sale. We decide to go down and buy a load of them and place them in our area so we can have a place to sit and talk after a day's work. The picnic table is great but not everyone can fit at it.

We jump in a truck and head down to the PX. The PX was the only store on the camp so it was always busy and the prices were good. We grabbed what chairs we think we need to make a good sitting area and head back. We place the chairs around the table and take a seat. Soon the rest of the truckers start to join us and the sitting area is created. We talked in the sitting area till a little past eight, everyone enjoying a quiet moment together. Everyone has some kind of drink and almost everyone has a smoke lit.

All of a sudden we hear a crash no more the 200 meters from our area. It was a rocket attack on the camp. There is another crash. It's a second rocket. The siren sounded from a distance. The choppers located right across the road from our sleeping area started up. Within minutes, the pilots were in the air and looking for whoever shot those rockets. There were people in helmets running for shelter in concrete bunkers. We waited to see if there would be a third rocket but there wasn't. After a while the siren stopped. Not long after that I decided to call it a night and headed to my room. Before I went to bed I cleaned my rifle. I made myself a promise that if at all possible I would clean my rifle every night. After all, what am I without my rifle but a target? After I finished cleaning my rifle I decided to watch a movie and go to sleep.

The next morning I woke up and did my usual routine. Wash, breakfast, and then off to work in our bus. I met up with Brad in the stores tent. He was putting drinks and snacks into a cooler. While he was doing that I decided to have a smoke. I took a minute while smoking and looked around the compound. I noticed that in the morning the heat wasn't so bad. The temperature was almost like our Canadian summers, around 20C. It was nice not to feel like a baked potato for a short time.

I notice the Bison and the LUVW that had been in the convoy with the suicide bomber. Sergeant Winchester didn't want anyone to go near the vehicles. The two vehicles had to have been covered in blood from that poor guy. Still have not heard if he is okay. I hope so. I am awakened from my daze by Brad yelling to me.

Brad – Anytime you want to join me, Jamie, is fine with me.

Brad starts to laugh in a manner only he can. It was a hardy deep laugh you would expect from the biggest kind of man. I quickly grab my rifle and hop in the truck. Brad has the cooler between the two seats. He opens it up and pulls out two bottles of water and passes them to me. Then he pulled out a small brown paper bag. He opened the bag and inside were packs of Gatorade crystals. The Gatorade was all the same flavour, blue.

Brad – I am sick of drinking just water. I need something with a little flavour. This is better than nothing. I heard they have different flavours ordered but your guess is as good as mine as to when we will get them.

Jamie – They brought in some protein bars for us.

Brad – Did you try them? I did and they are horrible. They are like honey and rice crisps mixed together. Nasty.

Jamie – Once again, nothing but the best for us, eh?

Brad – I know, man. The soldiers in the other countries must look at us and think to themselves, holy shit.

We both laugh.

Jamie – What about the British? Did you see some of their vehicles? I know ours are green but at least we have some protection. The British have some trucks that don't even have a windshield.

Brad – I know, man, that's crazy.

Jamie – But I guess they are just like us. You make do with what you have.

Brad – That's the truth, brother.

Brad takes his right hand away from the steering wheel and points a fist in my direction. I reach out my left fist and punch his fist. The rest of the day we went from place to place filling up reefers and coolers, or generators and light stands. We had a clipboard with a list of who needed fuel and we provided that. Our list was pretty long so it took us the whole day. If was a good first job for me as it gave me a chance to see the entire base which was bigger than I thought it would be and very well guarded and surrounded by a large wall. If anything tried to attack us there were choppers standing by ready to take off and find whatever it was.

I got to see the hospital and thought to myself, 'That's one place I hope I never see the inside of.' I got to see where the ammo was located and the laundromats and where some of the Afghan people work on the base. I saw that there were soldiers from all over the world here and also civilians who were making a lot more money than the soldiers.

I remember talking to a sergeant from the American army who told me he and his men had to guard an oil rig once. They were protecting the civilians who worked on the rig. The civilians were making $15,000 or more a month than the soldiers. Now how can that be fair, I ask you?

After the last name was checked off our list, Brad and I headed down to the far end of the camp to fill up our truck. Fuel is kept in large fuel bags that sit on top of the ground. You always end the day by filling up your truck for the next guy's camp refueling. Once the truck was topped up we headed back to the compound and dropped off the truck and headed into the driver's room to see who was there and find out what we were doing the next day. Turns out not much going on but more camp refueling and someone else was doing that. That means I will come to the driver's room and maybe end up doing some maintenance on the trucks here in the compound.

That night after supper I decided to give my parents a call to let them know their baby boy is okay. I smiled at how excited Mom was to hear from me. She tells me she heard about the suicide bomber on the news. She asked if I knew the guy who was hurt. I told her I didn't know the guy who was hurt, but I did have some friends who were closely involved. I guess she was going to find out sooner or later how dangerous it was for me over here. I just wish it was a little later.

My father got on the line and asked me how I was doing. I told him I was okay and we talked about what I did that day. We finished our talk with them both saying they were proud of me and then I hung up the phone. I guess my first full day of work had tuckered me out because all I wanted was to go to bed. So I took a shower and went to my room. No sitting outside tonight. I brush down my weapon and turn in.

I woke up and the room was dark. I check my watch. 3:15 a.m. I realize I have to pee badly. I jump out of my bunk and put on my desert boots. No time for my pants, my shorts or my weapon. I have to go too bad. I step out of my sleeping Mod and start running towards the bathroom closest to me. I get halfway there and I realize I am not going to make it. I have to go right here. I guess my body just wasn't used to me drinking that much water. I am still trying to get used to the heat of Afghanistan so I drink a lot of water and because of that I now find myself standing in my boxers peeing between the bathroom and the Mod tent. Once I finished I quickly got back to my bunk. Luckily, nobody saw me. The next day during breakfast I heard Pat talking about how he had to get out of bed at 2 a.m. to go for the worst piss of his life. I guess I wasn't the only one losing sleep over a full bladder.

After breakfast we headed to the driver's room. The chairs by the computers quickly filled up and people begin to check their email. Even if it was the smallest of emails, it was nice to hear from back home. Other guys were jumping onto land-line phones and hooking themselves up with a CSN line for a free phone call to loved ones. Others sat and waited for their turn.

Today was the day they were going to put satellite TV in our driver's room. Some of us hoped we would be able to get the UFC (Ultimate Fighting Championship) fights when we got the satellite, others hoped for playoff hockey. No matter what we got it would be better then what we had, nothing.

The TV guys are about 45 minutes hooking everything up. When they finished they passed the remote to Sergeant Healey and walked out the door. The sergeant started going through the channels to see what he could find. Every time he selected a channel it would not allow him to view it. He had no luck with channel after channel. But there he sat going through each one. After about an hour he turned to the other sergeant.

Sgt. Healey – We've got more than 300 channels and I've found three that work. Two of them were porn and one was a soccer channel. I hate soccer and I can't watch porn with a bunch of men.

Everyone starts to laugh

Sgt. Healey – I guess I could come up here after hours for some time alone.

Everyone laughs again.

It's after lunch and when I get back to the driver's room I am met at the door by Cody Murphy. He asks if I want to come to clothing stores with him. He was hoping to get himself a laundry bag. I thought it would be a good idea for me to go since I didn't know where it was. Cody told me it was close enough that we could walk so that's what we did. With his new laundry bag in his pocket, Cody stepped out of stores with a smile. We were walking back to the compound when Cody stopped me and pointed to something on our right.

It was a large crane about 100 meters in height, carrying a large C container. The Afghan driver slowly brought the container around and lowered it onto the back of a large jingle truck. Another Afghan man jumped up onto the top of the container and unhooked the cords that were hanging from the crane. After the cords were unhooked, the Afghan on the C container started yelling to the guy driving the crane. The guy driving the crane would always wait until the other guy grabbed onto the cords so he could be lowered to the ground. But this time the guy driving the crane had a different idea. I don't know what those two guys were yelling at each other but when the guy on the C container grabbed hold of the cords the driver quickly raised the cords up until the man was at the top of the crane.

Cody – Holy shit, man! If he falls he's dead.

We stood there, our eyes fixed on the dangerous action going on before us. Nothing we could do; if he falls he falls. All we can do is watch as one man's life is placed in the hands of another. The driver lowered the cords halfway down and begun to swing the cords from left to right. We could hear the man on the container screaming as he swung back and forth, side to side. Then the driver stopped swinging the cords and lowered the man to the ground. I couldn't believe what I had just seen. If this had happened in Canada someone would be going to jail. But here it's just another day. After it was over we headed back to the compound, eager to tell the story to the boys.

In the driver's room I check the job list for tomorrow and see that I am on the luggage run with Dave. Another day in the camp. I wonder when I will get my chance to drive outside the wire?

6 a.m. Another day and I wake and do my morning routine. Breakfast was extra good today because Pat told me about the scrambled eggs with everything. He said the cooks had diced peppers, onions and mushrooms ready to go into the eggs if they were asked. Pat said you can even ask for egg whites only. When he said that it brought me

back to a time when I was home from the army and in the kitchen. I tried to tell her yolks are not that good for you. But Mom thought it was a waste of food and then she went into her talk about how there are people in the world who would kill for those yolks.

Well, Pat wasn't kidding. The eggs with everything were great and I remember saying I might have to have them every morning I am here. I would like it to be every day but as a trucker you know you won't get that chance. Some of us will be outside the wire for weeks at a time. Funny how there will be people on this base who will get paid more than me and also get promoted out of this tour, but never have to leave the comfort of their air conditioned office.

After breakfast I decide to walk to work. It wasn't that far and I was pretty full after eating those eggs. I found Dave in the stores room sucking back a can of Red Bull like it was the first beer on a hot summer day.

Dave – Me and you on luggage today, Jamie ole buddy.

Jamie – Oh yes

We grab a few bottles of water and a snack. I went with a pack of Pop Tarts. We each jumped in an HLVW and headed out of the compound and down to the runway. Our job was pretty simple. We just pick up luggage for the people coming in on the flights. We parked our trucks by the old hanger I remembered from when I first arrived. I jumped out of my truck and decided to get in with Dave. Turned out Jason was joining us too. Me and Dave were looking after the luggage while Jason had the small jingle bus to carry the soldiers that came off the flight.

Jamie – What's up, brother?

Dave – This is it, man. Wishing I was anywhere but here.

Jamie – I hear that.

We're quiet for a few minutes.

Jamie – I don't think I will ever get used to the heat.

Dave – Or getting blown up.

Jamie – Well, I can't say that has ever happened to me.

Dave – I saw it happen, man, it was fast. It was like, before you even knew what was going on, it was just BOOM! And you hear people yelling on the radio. But for me that wasn't the bad part. It was when I was trying to get back to base, man. Freaking Bison caught fire and I couldn't get out of my seat. Thank God for Sarge or I'd be dead.

I watched as Dave drifted off into space when he finished his sentence. It was like he'd just realized he could have died at that moment in the Bison. Then as fast as he drifted off he came to again.

Dave – Man, I don't know if I can handle going out again.

I didn't know what to say. I can't blame him for not wanting to go out. It was a very close call and it was his first trip outside the wire too. Just goes to show that you never know when you can get hit. It could well be on your first convoy. We finished our tasking by noon so after lunch we hung around the supplies tent. Dave was feeling a lot better. I thought he was acting like his old self again.

Dave is a big fan of the WWE (World Wrestling Entertainment), so while walking around drinking a bottle of water he decided to do his best impression of Triple H (Paul Michael Levesque is a wrestler whose ring name is Triple H). Once Dave did his impression and we all had a few laughs more guys joined in, all trying to do their best impressions of Triple H. It made for some great videos. We kept doing this until we heard this music playing off in the distance. The music came from a small car that had entered our compound. It was Afghan music and it was so bad. The car pulled up in front of the driver's room and four Afghan men got out with brooms and mops. They were there to clean the driver's room. They kept the music going until one of the sergeants came out and told them to turn it off. We stayed in the stores tent while they cleaned, listening to the radio and telling stories. After almost an hour the four men came out and got back into their car. The crappy music quickly came back on and the car started to drive out of the compound.

The first thought that pops into my head is, 'What kind of job did they do on our driver's room? How clean is it?' I had to find out for myself. I started to walk across the compound to the driver's room. I soon realized I was not alone. Everyone with me in the stores tent had the same thought. I stepped in through the doorway with the boys right behind me. I was only one step inside and I could smell it already. Body odour. You could smell these guys through the whole room. One of the sergeants asked me to open the back door to get some air in so I quickly walked through the room and opened the door. The sun hit my face and I squinted my eyes as I walked out and blocked the door open with a large brick I found there. I also found a soccer table game. I told the boys and without delay they started a game. While they played, I stepped back inside the room because I still wanted to see what kind of a cleaning job those Afghan men did. The floors were now covered with streaks of dirty water and the room still smelled like an old guy's feet. It didn't help that it was super hot that day and with the doors open our air conditioner would not be much good. We played games out back the rest of the day until the Doc came over with the 'to do list' for tomorrow. I was on security detail for the market. I was happy with that. Not only do I get my first crack at being outside the wire but I might get a chance to go to the market too.

That night after I had supper I thought about phoning Vanessa. I wanted to but I stopped myself from doing so. 'She is better off without me,' I think to myself. Better to end it now in case something happens to me. Or what if I end up like one of those soldiers you hear about. A soldier who loses everything to someone they are living with. Or a soldier who comes home to a spouse who is cheating on them with the neighbour.

So instead of calling Vanessa, I called the house where I lived in Edmonton. I talked to Foley and I told him I needed movies. He told me he would do up a care package and put some movies in there for me. I thanked him and told him to say hi to the boys at the BN while he told me to say hi to the boys here. The rest of the night I sat with a few of the boys and we talked about how great it would be to have just one beer right now. But it was a dry camp and no beer for us.

Later on in the tour some country singers are coming to the camp to put on a show for us and we will get two beers each. Nice. Six months and you get two beers. I think we deserve more than two beers. Two is better than none, I guess. Trying to look positive here!

I have to have a shower, clean my rifle and go to bed. Lying in bed I realize I have to go to the PX tomorrow. I need to buy something to watch on my DVD player besides the two movies I have: *The Longest Yard* and *Blade*.

* * *

I woke in the morning before my alarm went off. It was like my body wanted to start the day. I got out of my bunk and did my routine with washing and breakfast. My eggs were great as usual and not as many people in the mess today. It's Sunday and I heard that on Sunday a lot of people on the camp get the morning off. It's called Sunday Routine. As truckers, we did not get too many Sunday Routines. There were always things to be fueled up or delivered.

After breakfast, I grabbed my gear and headed up to our compound. When I got there Scott had the back door of the Bison opened and was checking everything out. Turns out he was going to be the driver for the security team going to the market today. That was good news to me. I was glad a buddy of mine was going with me for my first step outside the wire.

I give Scott a hand getting the Bison ready. Soon other soldiers from different trades begin to gather around our Bison. They are the rest of the security party. One of the soldiers was a Master Corporal (MCpl.) who would be the leader of the team. The MCpl. was a young guy from Nova Scotia named Brown and his trade was a maintainer (mechanic).

MCpl. Brown got the team together and gave us a quick brief on what would happen at the market and who would be doing what job. He explained that we would leave in the Bison and go out the main gate of the camp. Then we would drive to the second gate that was manned by the Afghanistan National Army (ANA). Once there, the Bison would stay parked on the road and one person would man the C6 machine gun in its turret. Two soldiers would then stand in the front and pat down and check the Afghan people as they entered the market. Other soldiers would stand behind and guard the first two soldiers. I was chosen to be the first guy, the one that did the checking. When I was given that job MCpl. Brown told me not to miss an inch on the body of the person I was checking.

Jamie – You mean I have to grab balls?

MCpl. Brown – Not an inch to be missed.

MCpl. Brown then explained that before any of this happens we would have to do a sweep of the area. The reason for the sweep is because Afghanistan is one of the most mined places in the world. So we would have to walk through the area and check for anything that looks suspicious. All the things that we have in this big beautiful world and we don't have something that can detect metal in the ground yet? We still have to send my stupid ass in to check?

After MCpl. Brown finished his little speech we all had a quick smoke and a drink of water and loaded into the back of the Bison. MCpl. Brown climbed up into the turret and Scott started our drive to the meeting point. The meeting point was where all the vehicles that were set to be in a certain convoy would meet. Let's say a convoy was set to depart at 0700. Well, in a convoy you would need a medic, a maintainer, security etc. A maintainer would have his own Bison in case there was a vehicle breakdown on route. The security force would have its own vehicle. All these people would be given a time to be at the meeting point. Once at the meeting point we would set up our communication system and get our vehicles ready for the convoy. Every convoy always had a trucker involved, because there was always a need for food, water or fuel in a Forward Operating Base (FOB).

At the meeting point there was another LAV that would be the protection for the Bison. Inside the Bison, MCpl. Brown passed me a pair of rubber gloves. I felt the Bison stop and watched as the back door dropped. We all quickly jumped out and formed an extended line. Once we were in the straight line we advanced forward keeping a sharp eye on the ground in front of us and where we stepped, always looking for something that didn't look right. We walked all around the area where the market would be set up. There were already tables set up there, just waiting to be covered with things that the Afghan people would be trying to sell to the soldiers from the base.

Once the area was clear, I moved back onto the road with the Bison and moved to the front. I watched as the gates opened and the Afghan people started to walk towards me. I took out my blue rubber gloves and put them on and waited for the first person to approach me. The first one stepped up to me and stood in front of me with his legs spread and arms out to his side. I started to check down each arm, his chest and back. Let's just say all the bases were covered. After checking around his ankles I stood up and then I realized that a huge line had formed behind him. I let him pass and the guy behind me had a metal detector and was whipping him down. I guess you can't be too careful.

Hundreds of people stood in front of me that morning, each standing in the same position waiting for me to check them over. With the market running and the body checking done I decided to head over to the Bison and have a smoke. As I stood by the Bison with Scott I saw another line up. This line up was made up of soldiers waiting to enter the market and see what deals they could get.

Scott – Maybe we should get in there and look around. This might be our only chance.

First thing we noticed in there were the DVDs. There were thousands of DVDs on sale. DVDs from brand new movies that were still in theatres as well as full seasons of television shows. There were large beautiful carpets and boxes of jewelry, gold and silver. Very cheap smokes, $3 a carton. Well, I had to get in on that. I decided to buy a lot of smokes. I was sure some of the boys would want them. I also bought full seasons of some of my favourite television shows. Something to relax with at night in my bunk.

With a few bags in hand, Scott and I headed back to the Bison. We sat there until 1100 hours, time for the market to end. All the soldiers made their way out of the market and the Afghan people packed up their things and headed out the gate. When all our guys were aboard the Bison, Scott drove us back to the compound. Every soldier in the Bison had at least one bag of goodies they'd bought at the market. It was good to see soldiers and Afghan people getting along. It helped me see that we are not that different.

Back in the compound all the soldiers from the security team went back to their units. I helped Scott clean out his Bison and refuel it. One of the rules of the compound was always refueling your vehicle after a tasking was complete. We then cleaned our rifles and checked to see our jobs for tomorrow. I was on a convoy. It was not a big one, just a trip out to a forward operating base and back. The base was not far, maybe 30 minutes away. I thought it would be a good starter for me. Jason was going with me. It would be his first trip outside the wire too.

That night, Scott was a little pissed off. Turns out he was on one of the computers tonight, just checking email and doing a little Facebook time. While he was online he came across a picture of his girlfriend. She was at a club and she was wearing a shirt that said, 'Single for a night.'

Scott – She is cheating on me. I know it.

Jamie – Well, you don't know that for sure.

Scott – What kind of woman wears a shirt like that while her boyfriend is overseas?

Mike – A bitch.

Scott wants to laugh but he can't even get himself to smile at what Mike said. But Mike was right. What kind of woman would put her boyfriend through that? It might have been meant as a joke but a soldier has enough to worry about overseas. He doesn't need grief coming from back home as well.

Jamie – Have you talked to her much?

Scott – I have talked to her but not much.

Jamie – Well, hear her side of the story before you give up on her.

It's getting late so I head to my bunk. Scott is close behind me and so is Jason. We all crash on each other's bunks. I take out my rifle and give it a quick wipe down. I figure it didn't hurt since I would be going on a convoy tomorrow. With my rifle cleaned, I lie back on my buck and Scott continued to pour his heart out to me and Jason about his feelings towards his girlfriend. He has one child with her, a young boy, looks just like Scott. It's too bad because he really wants to build a family with her. But if her actions don't tear his family apart his jealousy will.

I don't remember what time I fell asleep but it was at least midnight. I'd wanted to go to bed early so I would be well rested for the morning. But it's okay. I had a brother in need of a friendly ear and for my brothers-in-arms there is nothing I wouldn't do.

5 a.m. was when I had my alarm set to go off and 4:50 was when I picked up my watch to check out the time. 'It's just as well to get up now,' I thought, so that's just what I did. I guess Jason heard me get up because I only had time to brush my teeth before he was out of his bunk.

Once we had finished our morning routines we jumped into one of the SUVs parked close to our sleeping quarters and headed up to the compound. We didn't bother to pack a lot of food to take on the convoy, just some bottles of water. It's not a long drive to where we are going but water goes with us everywhere. It's crazy. I drink so many bottles of water a day and still my pee is dark yellow. For the amount of water I consume in a day my pee should be as white and clear as water. But no, it's dark yellow.

* * *

The place we were going was called the PRT (Provincial Reconstruction Team).The PRT was a smaller version of the main camp and located about thirty minutes away. It had one kitchen and fewer soldiers. Our main camp was set up with an airstrip for planes to land, tents for more than 5,000 soldiers, and included three kitchens, a gym, and a computer room for the troops. I'd heard the mess hall at the PRT had really good food. Judging by the time, it looked like we would be getting there around dinner time so I guess we will get a chance to try out the food.

Jason wants to drive so he gets behind the wheel, which makes me the radio man in the passenger seat. Our vehicle is an LUVW. A pretty good vehicle to say the least. From first glance it looked like the army's version of a Jeep TJ. Put it into four wheel drive and she could go almost anywhere. But you had to be careful because like the Jeep TJ she could be easily tipped over. As I sit in the LUVW I get an ugly feeling deep in my stomach because the vehicle has no up armour on it and the windshield has two bullet holes in it, right in line to where I was sitting.

Jason – Well, this feels safe.

We break into laughter as Jason starts the engine and I fire up the radio. When we arrive at the convoy meeting area there are vehicles there already. They are lined up in the same position they will be in while driving in the convoy. Everyone is doing final checks on their vehicles, equipment, or loads. The communications guy is walking from vehicle to vehicle checking the radios to make sure they are all working properly. It is crucial that each radio works so that vehicles can stay in touch with each other in order to pass on what is going on and to share any signs of danger.

The night before we had been told our position in the convoy. We were the second vehicle so that's where we headed. Jason pulls the LUVW to the front of the line. We pass other vehicles. Between the first and third vehicle there is a space. The guy who was third knew we were coming and left a space. Jason pulls into the space and shuts off the engine. We both get out. I check to make sure the doors in the back are locked, they are. Got to make sure of that. Don't want to be driving down the streets of Kandahar city and have some Afghan run up to our vehicle and open one of those doors. Bad way to get hit by a suicide bomber. It's not too long before the communications guy jumps into our LUVW and gets our radio working.

Communications guy – There ya go. Your communications is good to go.

Jamie – Thanks, man.

The word gets passed down that there will be an O group in ten minutes at the front vehicle. The O group is a chance for the convoy commander to talk to everyone and explain the route we are taking and what actions we will take when hit by certain situations, such as suicide bombers, attacks from the side or rear, or if our vehicles get separated. We call these our 'actions on.' Once the convoy commander is finished his little speech and all questions are answered we head back to our trucks and put on our gear. We put on our frag vest and tack vest, along with our helmet and safety glasses. We were always told to keep the chin strap on our helmet done up but I never like to do that. I remember back to when I was a kid and watched John Wayne movies with my dad. I remember how John Wayne would never do up his chin strap and I always thought that was cool. So since I knew no one would see how I was dressed, I let it hang there just like the Duke did.

As we sat there waiting for the convoy commander to radio to all trucks that we are moving now a sandstorm started. It was a full on sandstorm. There was no warning. It just came out of nowhere.

Jason – Well, where the heck did this come from?

Jamie – How did it come on so fast?

Crazy or not, here it was. This trip just keeps getting better and better. In a vehicle with no up armour and now in a sandstorm. Perfect!

We take a quick drive over to the main gate. We give the guys on gate duty a wave as we pass by. We knew that in those waves there is more than just 'Goodbye.' There is also a 'Be safe out there' and 'Come back alive.' We keep driving and I see the area where the market was set up. I tell Jason about how I had to search people as they came into the market and how I could not miss an inch. Jason starts to make barfing noises.

As we passed through the second gate I saw the Afghanistan National Army (ANA) soldiers who were on gate duty. They looked mean in the face but not in the body. First thought that goes through my head when I look at one of the guys is, 'Can I beat him in a fight?' The longer I stare at him the more I think, 'Yep.'

After the second gate, we come to a 'T' junction in the road. That road was the highway, the only paved road around the base. The ANA have the right side of the road blocked off so we can enter the highway and turn left. All vehicles make the left turn onto the highway. When the last vehicle enters the highway the driver radios to the convoy commander that he is on the highway and we are on our way.

Our convoy keeps to the speed limit and we also drive down the center of the highway, causing most vehicles we pass to pull over to the side of the road to let us by. For the first few kilometers there is not much to see. A few people are standing on the side of the road and there was a shepherd with his sheep off in the distance. There was desert as far as you could see. When I say desert I don't mean that there was nothing but sand. It was more like the land had nothing more to give; nothing could grow here. I guess it's the long term effects of a country that has been at war for so many years.

After those first few kilometers we came to a bridge that had a gate going across it and it was being guarded by the ANA. As our front vehicle approached the gate the ANA soon realized who we were and opened the gate. As we passed by the gate there was something that was a bit of a shock to me. One of the ANA soldiers was a young child. He could not have been any older than ten or eleven tops. The young soldier was fully dressed in an ANA military uniform and carrying an AK47 rifle. I quickly thought of Avery and pictured him in this young soldier's shoes. Children that age should not be on gate duty with a weapon. They should be playing sports, video games or just playing. I soon realize that the children of Afghanistan have to grow up much faster than I did.

After we crossed the bridge and traveled a few kilometers further along the highway we entered Kandahar city. Here, there were many people on each side of the road. The road had a concrete divider that ran down the center of it all the way through the city. All along the side of the highway were small stores with things for sale. These were not like North American stores. These buildings all looked like they should be condemned. They were dirty and worn down and looked like they had been broken into many times. Knowing that the Taliban take what they want, when they want, from these people I would think that every building in this city has been broken into countless times. Everything from crafts and clothes to food and drink was for sale. You could find anything from tools and vehicle parts to dead animals hanging in front of the buildings. To me, most of the animals looked like skinned cats.

When an army convoy like us came through the city, most Afghan people would stop and stare. There were kids running out and stopping at the side of the road to wave at the big green trucks as they passed by. Vehicles crowded with people passed on the other side of the divider. People were riding on the roofs of cars, or hanging off the backs of trucks. I wonder if the Afghan people ever make jokes about Canada and its green vehicles and equipment. Some people ran in from the left side of the highway and crossed over to jump up on the concrete divider and wave at the passing convoy. Not a good thing to do to a nervous soldier. Could make a person pretty jumpy.

Jason – I don't like the way people run up to the side of the vehicle. Makes me think of suicide bombers.

Jason was right. That's a good way for an Afghan person to get shot and how can a guy over here take a chance? Over here, there are suicide bomber attacks all the time and I would rather be sorry for killing an innocent man than letting me or Jason get ourselves killed.

Carrying on down the road, now close to our destination, I realize that not all the people in the city like us. In the matter of twenty seconds I counted three rocks that hit the side of the truck. Maybe it was kids, but something told me it wasn't. Some bangs, you think it's just a rock, but sometimes you think it could be a grenade. You try to put it out of your mind. You stare at the vehicle in front of you and listen to the radio so you know your convoy is alright.

Our convoy pulls the vehicles in tight formation while we are in the city. It helps keep the suicide bombers from entering our convoy. We don't let anyone in our convoy. As we near the gate of the camp I see there is only one narrow path going in. Large piles of dirt are staggered along the path. This is to stop suicide bombers from sending a speeding car or a large truck to ram the gate. Jason follows the vehicle in front of us all the way around the camp to a small parking space where we park in two rows. I always liked it when we parked our vehicles in rows. There is something comforting about being able to get in between two rows of vehicles for cover from both sides.

We dismounted from our vehicles. The Bison in our convoy opened its back door so people could exit. There was one HLVW in our convoy. The driver of that vehicle did not park with us. He was off unloading his truck. The convoy commander gathered everyone in the convoy and said we would be heading back to camp in one hour. It was almost noon and time to eat. Jason must have been thinking the same thing because he quickly turned to me.

Jason – Dinner time, bitches.

I couldn't help but laugh. The kitchen wasn't much to look at but there was no shortage of food for the soldiers. It was all you could eat. After I finished I looked in the cooler in the back to find a dessert, perhaps some of that good Afghan yogurt. I was in luck. They had some here. They didn't have it in the main camp right now but they had it here. Well, now I like this mess more than the one on our camp.

After we finished eating, Jason and I kind of got zoned out on the television they had mounted in the corner. I don't think it was because it was a television, but for the first time in a while we got to watch TSN (The Sports Channel). I remember watching TSN in the morning before school with my dad. We were Leafs fans but at the time our team was out. So I thought being posted to Edmonton and with my Leafs not in the playoffs why not cheer for the Oilers? After eating a great meal, I now got to see that the Oilers made it to the playoffs.

Jason – Oilers are in the playoffs.

Jamie – Yep, guess I will have to cheer for them since my team is out.

Jason – That's because you're a Leafs fan, man. Let it go, man.

Jamie – Never, my dad would kill me.

We get up from the table and made ourselves a coffee and then headed outside to the smoking area for an after dinner smoke. Nothing like that after dinner smoke. I sat there, enjoying a moment where I could just sit and relax. I listened to Jason explain to me how much he missed the homemade poutine his mother used to make him. Funny, I think every boy thinks their mother is the best cook. I know I did, still do.

I remember when we were kids and we would spend the winter days and most of the nights riding on our parents'

Skidoos. We would ride for hours along the cabin trails. We stopped when we saw the cabin windows covered with steam because we knew when that happened my mother was making French fries and she was making them in her large cast iron black pot. I don't know why but food always tasted better in that pot.

It felt so hot sitting there having a smoke with Jason. The sun was beaming directly on me and there was no shade to be found. Every now and again you could feel a slight breeze but it wasn't the cool breeze from a fall day. This breeze felt as though someone had placed a hot hair dryer in front of your face. All you felt was warm air, and sometimes dust in your face. The dust was a bad part because you were always sweating and the blowing dust would stick to your forehead. Soon the hour was up and it was time for us to prepare for the trip back to the camp. Jason and I tossed our butts in a butt can, grabbed our rifles, and headed to our truck. We quickly put our vests and helmets back on. Then all the people in the convoy gathered together for a quick meeting before we hit the road. Seemed like everyone was ready to go so without further delay we jumped into our vehicles. Before we started to move there was a quick radio check; communications was always important.

The drive back to the camp was not much different from the drive in. The city was still crawling with people along with many vehicles speeding up and down the streets. There were also people riding around in carts pulled by donkeys. There was this one guy riding in his cart and I guess his donkey wasn't moving as fast as he liked. So the guy was swiping this donkey in the butt with a stick, trying to make him move faster.

It took us about forty minutes to get back to the main gate of our camp. We stopped just before we entered the camp so we could unload our weapons. This was something everyone had to do before they entered the camp. After the last vehicle was through the gate the driver radioed the convoy commander to let him know that everyone was safe.

Jason and I headed back to the transportation compound. Once there, we re-fuelled our truck and took out any extra kit, including ammo, as well as our radio and our cooler for keeping bottled water cold. After our vehicle was looked after it was on to cleaning our rifles. This was normal work once you finished a convoy. The convoy was not complete until you had your vehicle ready for the next time it had to go outside the wire. We always had to be ready. You never could tell what kind of mission would pop up so we had to keep our trucks prepped at all times.

Now that the truck was ready for the next guy, we headed in to talk to the warrant officer and our lieutenant. They always wanted to talk to soldiers returning from outside the wire. I guess it was just to check and see how the convoy went. I can understand why they wanted to know. After all, they were the bosses and they needed to know.

By the time Jason and I were finished for the day the driver's room was empty. Lucky for us there was another small SUV left so we jumped in that and headed down to the sleeping area. At the sleeping area some of the boys were gathered around the sitting area smoking and listening to music. One of the boys had his MP3 player hooked up to a speaker placed in our sitting area. The music playing was classic country. Merle Haggard was singing *Working Man's Blues* when I stepped out of the truck. For a short moment I felt like we were on the patio of Dad's cabin and all guitars were out. For that short moment, I was home.

I stayed in my room the rest of that night. Maybe it was because I was missing home and thinking of Dad's cabin that I decided to stay in my little room and watch a movie on my DVD player. The movie was Tombstone, my favourite movie. Val Kilmer playing Doc Holiday was so great. He had some of the best one-liners I have ever heard in a movie. My favourite was 'I'm your huckleberry.' Love it.

That night as I finished writing in my journal, I thought about Vanessa. I wonder if she has been on any dates with anyone since I have been gone. After all, I didn't give her the best goodbye when I left. Why would she want to be with me? I was a jerk to her. No way has she not been on at least one date. I bet that guy is a dick too. If she thinks I am going to meet this guy she is crazy. I can see us now. He puts out his hand to shake mine and I just snap and punch him in the face. Why am I getting so worked up? I'm lying in my bunk, pissed off. Wonderful, I now have the ability to piss myself off without anyone else being in the room. I must be a delight to be around. I ended up falling asleep that night not knowing who I was more pissed at, me or Vanessa.

The next day after breakfast I decide to hitch a ride in a bus with the boys. Anyone not already gone on convoy could always get a ride on the bus. The bus pulled into the transportation compound and parked. One by one we all got off. And there, on the flat bed of a sixteen ton truck, sat the vehicle that had been hit by the suicide bomber. The vehicle from Dave's convoy. The vehicle was in bad shape like it had just been in the worst accident ever on the highway. No one spoke. We all just stared at it for a moment. I am sure we were all thinking the same thing and maybe for the first time it really sank in.

This is not like any other tour Canada has been on in a long time. This was no peacekeeping mission. This was a real war and there was a very good chance we would all be involved in attacks of our own. For some, there was a touch of excitement, but for all there was a sense of fear and thoughts of not making it home alive. The first thing I thought about was who would miss me. I pictured the people who would come to my funeral and how it would play out.

Sergeant Winchester tells us all to get back and not to look at the beat up vehicle. He walked over and jumped behind the wheel of the sixteen ton truck carrying the busted vehicle and drove it out of the compound and out of our sight. At the time we all wondered where he was going with that vehicle. I turned away and headed inside the driver's room. I thought about getting on a phone and maybe calling Mom or Vanessa, but all the phones were in use. Every soldier loves to hear the friendly voice of a loved one at home.

Plan B was going to be the computers and maybe check my email. But once again I had no luck. All the computers were in use. The boys were looking up Chuck Norris facts. Norris is an American martial artist and actor. Seemed like a funny way to pass the time. Even the soccer table out back was in use. I decided to head over to the stores tent, maybe grab a muffin and water and after that maybe check out one of the trucks. As I find myself a muffin, someone finds me. It was Brad.

Brad – Jamie, you want to come do camp refueling with me?

Brad was on camp refueling with Stan Green, but Stan had gone to the MIR (Medical Inspection Room) again. Stan was known to the platoon as more of a problem than a help. When Canada sends people overseas they send over a certain number of soldiers. But when some of the soldiers they send are people who run to the doctor every time they have a little sniffle then it makes the work load harder on the rest of us. Stan seemed to always be sick.

Jamie – I thought you were on camp refueling with Stan

Brad – I was, but you know where he went this morning.

Jamie – Don't tell me he went to MIR again today.

Brad – Yep, but this is a good one.

Jamie – Okay, what is his story this time?

Brad – He was saying today that he got up early and had a shower. After the shower he took a Q-tip and used it to clean out his ears. That's where things went wrong. He said he pushed the Q-tip in too far and he thinks he might have busted his ear drum.

Jamie – Oh my God! That is one of the dumbest things I have ever heard.

Brad starts laughing.

Jamie – I mean it, man. He stabbed himself in the brain with a Q-tip.

Brad laughs even louder now.

Jamie – Ah, whatever, man. I will do it with you.

Camp refueling was a long one today. It seemed like every place on the camp was on the list and they were all almost empty. That can happen sometime if the guys who were on camp refueling before you don't have many people on their list. I don't want to say that it could be because they skip their stops. But you can understand why sometimes you can't help but think it. The truck we were driving had a ten thousand litre tank, but we had to go back and fill it up three times. Plus it seemed that the sun had no mercy today. It just belted down rays like they were going out of style. There was no escape from the heat. The trucks we used on the camp did not have air conditioners like the up armour ones we drive outside the wire. These were just like the ones I rode around in as a kid where the only cool breeze you felt came when the window was down. But here there was no cool breeze. Although there was a breeze from time to time it was never a cool one.

When we finished the last spot on our list we drove down to the far end of the camp and topped up our refuelled one last time. Then we headed back to the transportation compound and parked the truck for the day. By the time we got there it was almost 6 p.m. and all the boys had gone back to the sleeping area. They only people left there were the lieutenant and the warrant officer. I walked over and checked to see what I was doing tomorrow. I was on a detail with Doug Miller. That sounded good. Doug and I were great friends.

Doug was always cool to talk to because he spent a lot of his life training to be a cage fighter. I was a big fan of the ultimate fighting championships (UFC) so being able to talk to someone like Doug was fun for me. When I watched UFC on television there were moves I didn't understand so I asked Doug to show me how to do them and he was more than willing to show me. Maybe it was fun for him to practice some moves on someone. Plus Doug was from Newfoundland just like me, and when you are from Newfoundland and you meet another Newfie you try and look out for each other.

The job for me and Doug was to meet up with an Afghan man driving a jingle truck refueler. We have to escort him to where we fill our refuelers, top him up, and then escort him out of the camp. Sounds like an interesting job.

That night, I called Mom and Dad. I just had to hear their voice and let them know I was okay. I kept thinking about the truck that was all beat up from the suicide bomber. I guess the word of that attack got back to Canada and my parents had seen it on the news. As I was talking to my parents the phone went silent and then I heard Dad come back on the line.

Dad –Sorry, buddy, but Mom is gone off crying. She is having a hard time with this.

Jamie – I know she is, Dad, we all are. But we will get through it. After all, we're Youngs.

Dad started to laugh. That was something he would always say to me. 'We're tough, Jamie. We're Youngs. I can still hear him saying it. I guess him hearing me say it made him smile, even if for a brief minute. I said goodbye to him and decided to call it a night. A quick shower and I was in my bunk.

I tried to watch a movie, but there was just no use. I was too tired to keep my eyes open. I remember turning on the movie and blinking and then the movie was close to the end. I blinked again and the main menu was playing. I opened my eyes long enough to close the DVD player that sat on the barrack box next to my bunk. My head plopped back on the pillow and I quickly passed out into a deep sleep.

I dream about my parents in a car crash. I see them in the front seats of their truck, sitting there dead and covered in blood and glass. The truck is also on fire. I yell to them but there is no sound. I yell again and again but it's like I am a mute. No sound comes from my lips.

I keep yelling over and over again until my eyes pop open and it's morning. I lie there and realize it was just a dream. My bed is wet. I must have sweated a lot last night. I'm tired this morning. That was not the best sleep I have ever had. Oh well, no time to complain. It's not like I can call in sick. That's Stan's job.

I sit up in my bed and stare at the tarp wall on the other side of my room. I wasn't thinking about anything. I just stared at the wall. After about five minutes of doing nothing I forced myself off the bunk and started my morning routine. At breakfast, I met up with Doug. He was eating his usual breakfast of fruits and grains. Doug always took good care of himself with eating right and exercising. It was paying off too. Doug was in great shape. I brought my breakfast tray over to his table.

Doug – Morning, brother. What's going on?

Jamie – Barely awake, but I'm here.

Doug – I hear you, man. I would love a day to just sleep in.

Jamie – I know what you mean. Been here almost a month. Sure could use a Sunday Routine.

Sunday Routine means that unless you have a tasking, you don't have to come to work until after lunch.

Doug – Yes! Sunday Routine! Why can't we have one? Everyone else seems to get one.

Jamie – Maybe we need to say something. If we don't have some kind of break the boys will start to snap at each other.

Doug and I thought it was a good idea to talk to the rest of the platoon to see what they think. But that will have to wait for now. We had to get to the transportation compound to get ready for our tasking for today. We finished up our breakfast and headed back to our sleeping area to grab what we needed. We needed all the gear we usually wore when we headed outside the wire. Although we were not going outside the wire we were going to be providing protection and for that we had to be locked and loaded.

The vehicle we would be using was a LUVW, the same as the one I used when I went to the PRT. Doug said he felt like driving so I jumped in the passenger seat and started to get the radio ready. Once our vehicle was ready to go we grabbed a few snacks and some bottled water and were on our way. We were told we had to be at the parking lot by the main gate for 0900. Once there, we had to meet up with the Afghan man driving the refueler truck.

Doug and I sat there waiting and watching jingle truck after jingle truck enter the large parking lot. There were soldiers guiding each truck as it entered the parking lot so they would not end up parking wherever they felt like and bunching up in the parking lot. Once a vehicle was parked, the drivers were told to shut off their engines and exit the vehicle. Then the drivers were searched and at the same time their trucks were searched. There were soldiers with trained dogs that were let loose to find what they could on each truck. Everything was checked. In this line of work you can't take any chances.

Doug was the first to notice the refueler jingle truck enter the parking lot.

Doug – That one looks like ours.

We got out of our vehicle and walked to the front of it. We watched as the vehicle entered and parked just off to our right. We both walked over holding our rifles in plain sight.

Jamie – I will cover you while you search him.

Doug – Why do I have to be the one to search?

Jamie – Because I did the market duty where I had to search each person as they entered. I have had my fill of searching, thank you.

Doug couldn't argue with me so he just shut up as we walked to the truck. The driver had the engine shut off. The Afghan man must have been through this before because he jumped out of his truck and walked over to us and spread his legs and held out both arms. I stood a few feet back from Doug as he searched this man. I made sure to keep an eye on them and never have Doug standing between me and the Afghan man.

Once Doug gave me the thumbs up telling me the guy was clean we had him stand there while Doug checked out his truck. When Doug was satisfied, we headed over to the guys with dogs and told them the truck was ready for them. Doug then joined me and the Afghan man and we stood there watching these very well trained dogs do their job. These dogs not only checked around the truck, but they got up inside the cab of the truck and then down under the truck. Those dogs checked every inch of the truck.

We get the thumbs up from the dog guy and without saying a word that Afghan guy left our side and quickly climbed back into his truck. Doug and I walked over to our truck. Doug jumped behind the wheel and I stood next to the truck with my door open. The Afghan man slowly drove his refueler up to us.

Jamie – I guess he knows he has to follow us.

Doug – Guess so.

I jump in the truck and we slowly exit the parking lot with the refueler behind us.

Jamie – Take your time, Doug, keep him close.

Slowly we travel to the other side of the camp; to the same place we come to fill our own refueler. Just before we enter the refueling area Doug stops and I get out. Doug carries on into the refueling area while I have the Afghan man follow me into the area and I guide him into position.

Once the refueler was in position I told the driver to shut off the engine. He did so and then got out of the cab of the truck and quickly climbed up onto the large tank of the truck. I moved over to work the fuel pump while Doug climbed up onto the tank with the Afghan man. I pick up the hose and carry it over to the truck and then I pass it up to Doug. The Afghan driver opens the cap on the tank and Doug places the hose in the hole and gives me the thumbs up to let me know they are ready for me to turn on the pumps. The Afghan driver decides to help Doug and holds the hose to keep it in place. When I get the thumbs up from Doug I give him thumbs up back and slowly turn on the pump. I don't want to turn it on too fast in case it comes out too quickly at the start and Doug can't hold on to it. Fuel starts to flow out of the hose and into the tank. Everything seems to be running smoothly. The fuel in the tank is now past the halfway mark.

And then suddenly without warning something goes wrong. The Afghan driver's watch strap comes undone and falls into the tank. As soon as this happens, the driver stands up and jumps into the tanker without a word. I watch in shock as the man jumps into the tank full of fuel. Not knowing what else to do, I shut off the pump. Doug stands up and places the hose to the side.

Doug – Oh my God! Jamie, what do I do?

I stand there in shock over what has just happened.

Doug – What if he dies in there, Jamie? Nobody is going to believe us when we tell them he jumped in. They are going to think we killed him.

Doug was right. If he dies, nobody will believe he jumped in. They are going to think we pushed him in there, then what? We are going to go to jail because this crazy guy went in after a watch. Doug and I stood there not knowing what to do. It's not like we could go in there after him. Then just as suddenly as he jumped in, I watched as two hands rose from the hole and the Afghan driver climbed out of the tank and picked up the hose like nothing had happened. It must have been at least one minute that passed while Doug and I just stared at this guy. He sat there holding the hose and waiting for the fuel to start pumping again.

Doug – Are you okay, man?

The Afghan driver looked up at Doug with bloodshot eyes and red coloured skin. He blinked his eyes over and over, not saying a word. I thought to myself 'I can't let the guy just sit there like this.' I got him to come down from the top of the truck and I took him to a bathroom not far from our area so he could wash himself. I didn't want the man to do any permanent damage to himself. I know if I didn't do this, he might have some kind of health issues in his future.

While the guy cleaned himself in the bathroom I returned to his vehicle and Doug and I finished filling his truck. Once it was filled, Doug locked the cap back on the tanker with a special zap strap. The reason why we do this is because when the truck arrives at its destination and the zap straps are missing then we know that fuel has gone missing. At first there were problems with Afghan men stealing the fuel, but with this simple method we had no other problems with stolen fuel.

Doug and I stood there long enough to finish a bottle of water each and in Afghanistan that didn't take very long. I wanted to have a smoke but I thought this wasn't the place for that. Not long after our bottles of water were gone, the Afghan driver arrived back at the truck. His eyes and skin were still red but he did seem a little better. I tried to explain to him that I would be happy to bring him to the hospital but he would have nothing to do with that. Seemed he was more interested in having one of our bottles of water. So I gave him some water and some food and a few smokes for his drive. He tried to light one right away but Doug quickly stopped him from doing that. With his truck filled, we were ready to lead him out of the camp. So the driver jumped back in his truck and started the engine. Doug took our LUVW outside the refueling area. I walked the jingle truck out of the area and up behind Doug. We slowly drove back to the main gate and watched as the jingle truck drove out the main gate and off the camp.

That night when I got back to the sleeping area I decided to get a shower right away. After seeing that guy covered in fuel I felt I needed one. Me and one of the supply technicians were walking back from the showers just shooting the shit when a siren went off. It's the siren they use when the camp is under attack. Someone went running by and yelled at us to get our asses moving to the bunkers! So me in my towel and shower slippers went flopping down to the tent area to at least get some pants on. When I got to the bunker it was full so I moved on to the next one, which was also full. Oh well. Better to get hit directly by the rocket than to be crushed under the concrete from the bunker! After a couple more rocket attacks on camp we discovered that by the time the air siren went off it was too late for a warning because the rocket had already hit the ground!

That night, lying in my bunk I kept expecting to hear the siren go off again or hear a rocket hit the ground close to me. But it never happened, and before I knew it I heard my alarm going off. Time to get up. Another day of fun in Afghanistan.

I get up and start my morning routine then get dressed and head to the mess to get some breakfast. Almost all the boys from my platoon were there getting something to eat. Something about a rocket attack can make you hungry, I guess. After breakfast we meet up at the sleeping area. John has the bus keys. His job today is driving Afghan people to different jobs around the camp. As we were driving up to our compound we passed by some Americans who are walking. Scott decides to open the bus window and hang half his body outside and start yelling.

Scott – BALL HOCKEY, BOYS! TIME TO START SOME BALL HOCKEY, BOYS!

Jamie – What are you doing, man?

Scott – Canada vs. USA in ball hockey.

All I could think to myself was what a great idea!

Jamie – Speaking of hockey, how is Edmonton doing in the playoffs?

Jason – They are still in it.

I get to the compound and lucked out as I get to be one of the first people on a computer. This is a good chance for me to check out my bank account and maybe pay some money on my credit card. The boys quickly fill the driver's room. Seems to be a lot more people here than usual. That means there are not too many people on convoy today.

I guess I should be thankful there are computers over here for us to use, but it took me over thirty minutes to put some money on my credit card. After that it was time for me to start my tasking. Dan is on this tasking with me. We are both driving HLVWs. Our job was easy, follow John in the bus.

John will be driving the people and Dan and I will drive the trucks carrying their kit. But this time we were not picking up people who were just arriving in Afghanistan. We are taking people down to the airstrip to catch a plane out of here. These people were going on leave. I was jealous that they were getting to leave this place for a while, but I would get my chance too. The luggage tasking didn't take that long. We were finished by lunchtime. After lunch, I spent the afternoon filling jerry cans with fuel. The count was eighty-five when we finished. A good day's work.

* * *

That night, I was lying in my bunk watching a movie when Doc the dispatcher came in to tell me some news. He told me the reason why we filled those jerry cans full of fuel today was because they needed to be taken to the PRT. They are running low on fuel out there and we don't have a refueler in good enough condition to be outside the wire. Plus, our refueler doesn't have armour on it yet. Doc also told me that I would be the driver of the truck that would be carrying those jerry cans.

I was a little nervous about driving a truck full of jerry cans of fuel so I asked for a good co-driver. Well, at least another trucker like me. But there were none available; they were all on taskings tomorrow. So my co-driver would be a supply tech.

Doc told me because we are so busy we don't have the manpower to place two truckers on every convoy. So people from other trades will now be our co-drivers. We won't know who we will be working with from day to day. I didn't like this idea and it's nothing against anyone from other trades. But it is nice to be working with other truckers when you're trying to do a job in a place like this. But what can you do but work with what you have?

I went back to the transportation compound and gave my truck a quick look over. Then me and some of the boys loaded the truck with the fuel cans, tied down the load, and parked the truck for the night. Afterwards, we sat around our sleeping area. John had the radio turned on and Jason pulled out a big pack of cigars so we sat back and listened to the music and smoked the night away.

All we could talk about was how great it would be to have a beer, even one a night. A bottle of water was good on hot days, but a beer was what we wanted at night and that was something we were not allowed to have.

When I got in my bunk I opened my barrack box and stared at the pictures I had taped to the back side of the cover. The pictures were of my parents and of Vanessa with Avery. I sure do miss them. I wonder what they were all doing right now. I could see Mom and Dad sitting on the couch watching a hockey game, and then Dad asking Mom what was for lunch. Vanessa always asked me if I needed anything. She found it hard to believe I never needed anything. I just needed her. Vanessa's last boyfriend was a jerk and split when Avery came along so I guess she is always trying to please me. She is not used to having someone in her life who just wants her for herself. I don't know if I can be that man. I do love Vanessa. I just don't know if I am ready to settle down, or if I am ready to be a father to Avery.

That night I had a horrible nightmare in which Vanessa and Avery were attacked in their apartment and Avery was kidnapped. The Taliban took him and killed her. I woke up and looked at my watch. It was five minutes to six, in five minutes my alarm would go off. I thought it was just as well to get up.

When I got to our compound there was a guy standing outside of the driver's room. I guess the reason I noticed him was because I didn't know him. At this time of day the only people I should be seeing in the compound are truckers like me. This guy was fully dressed too; he had his frag and tack vest on along with his eye protection. The only thing missing was his helmet but it wasn't too far away. He was holding it in his right hand. Before saying anything I looked at his rank: Corporal.

Jamie – How's it going?

Unknown Soldier – Not bad. I was told to be here to be someone's co-driver.

Jamie – Well, I just might be your driver.

I open up the driver's room door and the first thing I notice is two other new faces. Turns out that the guy I just talked too is not the only co-driver today. I tell the WO about the guy who was here to be a co-driver and the WO tells him to take a seat with the other two guys.

Jamie – Hey WO, you mean we don't get two truckers per vehicle anymore?

WO Baker – No, there are too many taskings coming down and we don't have enough truckers to put two per seat. We have two truckers at every forward operating base. Plus truckers have to do camp duties.

Jamie – Well, maybe the camp duties need to be done by someone else. WO, you can't work the boys hard every day. People will start dropping on you.

The WO takes a step closer to me.

WO Baker – Just what do you expect me to do? We have a job to do. We are soldiers. We are told to do something and we do it.

Jamie – A good soldier does what he is told. But a warrior knows the difference between what's right and what's wrong.

I head over to my truck and give the engine one more check and then I give my load another check. While I am doing that I am joined by the guy I spoke with outside the driver's room. I guess he was going to be my co-driver for the day. I got a cooler and filled it with bottled water, pop, and a few snacks and I placed the cooler in the cab of the truck. Then I give my rifle a check over. I also get a radio to go in the truck so we can talk with the rest of the convoy.

The whole time I am doing these things my co-driver is standing there looking around. But it's not like it's his fault. This guy has never been on a convoy before so he doesn't know what should be done before we leave. Even though we truckers are getting a co-driver we aren't really getting a helping hand; we are getting students. Once my truck was ready and everything seemed good, I looked down at my watch.

Jamie – Time to go.

My co-driver quickly climbed up into the cab of the truck. I grab my gear and toss it up into the cab. I turn to Pat and Mike who were sitting there having a smoke.

Jamie – See you soon, boys.

I like to say 'See you soon' because it helps me put a thought in my head: I will make it back. Pat and Mike each hugged me like a brother.

Mike – Be safe, man.

With that, I climbed into the cab of the truck and started the engine and was gone in a cloud of dust. We drove up to the meeting area and I soon found my spot in the convoy. Once I was parked, I shut off the engine and told my co-driver to go find the Sig (Signals) guy and make sure our radio was working properly. While he was gone I thought to myself 'I need some good music in my truck.' Tonight I should go to the PX and get me a MP3 player and a speaker for inside the truck. My co-driver shows up with the Sig guy so I decide to exit the truck and have a smoke while they work.

It's fifteen minutes before our start time. We head to the front of the convoy so the convoy commander can give everyone a brief on where we are going and the route we will be taking. Once the brief was done and there were no questions from anyone we all jumped back into our trucks. I put on all my gear, but didn't do up the chin strap on my helmet. I knew if the WO found out about it he would tear a strip out of me, but for now I'm still John Wayne.

The day was going good and the convoy made it to the PRT without any problems. My co-driver tried his best to take pictures while he listened to the radio. I can understand his excitement. I was just like him when I first went off the camp. For a lot of soldiers this one convoy trip off the camp would be the big story to tell when they got home. But for a trucker, it was just another day.

At the PRT, it took no time to unload all the jerry cans of fuel. There were soldiers there waiting for me and they were more than happy to lend a hand. Within one hour we were all ready to leave the PRT and make our way back to our camp. We start up our vehicles and after a quick radio check we were on the road again. Everything was going well until we got to the last bridge before the main camp. I remember this bridge because it was where I had seen the young boy in an ANA uniform.

Suddenly our front vehicle was hit by an IED.

I didn't see the vehicle get hit but I heard the explosion. With the first truck down, a Bison came up to help the drivers and protect them if they were still alive. The rest of the vehicles pushed forward and closed the distance between each truck. As soon as the Bison got there it came under machine gun fire from its left. But the machine gun fire was only part of the problem. There were also rockets being shot at the Bison and other vehicles in the convoy. One of the LAVs in our convoy quickly came forward to help the Bison. Both the LAV and the Bison fired back until the drivers were taken from the front vehicle and placed in the Bison.

Within twenty minutes the fire fight was over and the convoy was in an all around defence mode. Every convoy has a wrecker, which is a vehicle that our maintainers use. It's like a tow truck and garage all in one. The wrecker quickly pulled up in front of the damaged vehicle. Within minutes, the two maintainers had the damaged truck hooked up to the back of the wrecker and we were ready to go. Word came back on our radio that we were ready to move.

Neither me nor my co-driver said a word the rest of the way back to camp. I think we were both in shock at what had just happened. But what do you say after something like that? I kept thinking about what had just happened and different ways it could have played out. Was there anything I should or could have done differently? I kept thinking about it until we were back at camp.

In silence, we passed through the main gates of the camp. My co-driver took his headset off and placed it to one side. I drove us back to the transportation compound and parked next to the refueler so I could refuel my truck for the next convoy. As always, the refuelled was parked next to the stores tent, and in the stores tent were Mike and Scott. No doubt they had heard of what happened in my convoy and wanted to see if I was okay.

Mike – How you feeling, brother?

Jamie – I will be okay after eight or nine smokes.

We all break into laughter.

Scott – You had us worried there for a second, man.

Jamie – It was a close call but I will be okay.

After my truck was refueled we headed back down to our sleeping area. When I got there the first thing I noticed were that there weren't many truckers around the smoking area. Most nights when I got back there would be plenty of truckers around, telling stories of what happened that day.

Jamie – Where is everyone?

Scott – A lot of us are out on convoys or placed in FOBs.

Mike – Yeah, truckers are always working over here.

Scott – We are outside the wire almost as much as the infantry. I think the infantry and us should be getting paid more than the big shots who just sit in their offices.

I agreed with Scott. People like us are in greater danger because we are often outside the wire and we also carry everything an Afghan person would want to steal. Most truckers who go on convoys carry food, water or fuel, all things that people want over here.

That night I felt like I needed to talk to someone back home so I called Vanessa. As soon as I heard her voice I forgot about what had happened that day. There was something about her voice that took me to another place, a safe place. I didn't do much talking. I left that to her. She spoke of how her day was going and how Avery was doing in school.

She also told me about how Avery wishes I was there and how he misses me. I told her to tell him I am doing well and I miss him too.

After she finished talking about her day I made up some excuse to say goodbye. I had nothing I wanted to talk about with her. I didn't want her to worry so I chose not to tell her about what had happened to me that day. I thought why worry her more than she already is. Not telling made it harder for me. I wanted to talk about it. I wanted people to know what I was going through over here. I just didn't want to be a burden to people and worry them more than they already were.

There was a package sitting on my bunk when I got back. It was from Mom. Inside were cookies she'd made, a few pictures from home, socks and underwear. She also had a note telling me she and Dad miss me and hope I am doing well. She said they were proud of me and that made me feel like a million bucks.

I had another nightmare that night. In the dream my parents' house was blown up by a bomb planted in the basement. I remember pulling up in front of the house and seeing it on fire. But instead of firemen stopping me from running inside to save Mom and Dad it was soldiers. Soldiers from my tour were stopping me and holding me back.

I woke up suddenly. I must have done a lot of tossing and turning in my sleep because when I looked all the covers had been kicked off the bed. I looked at my watch. It was five minutes to six. In five minutes my alarm would go off so I thought it was just as well to get out of bed and start my day. I already knew what I was doing.

My tasking today was driving an HLVW to the PRT and my load was boxes of bottled water. I didn't mind that job. I'd been to the PRT before and I knew they had the kitchen with the good yogurt. Maybe I'd be lucky enough to get some while I was there.

I got out of my bunk and did my usual morning routine then headed up to the transportation compound. At the compound a few guys were standing outside the door of our driver's room with all of their PPE (personal protective equipment) on.

No doubt in my mind that one of these guys was my co-driver. I didn't bother to talk to any of them. I figured I'd find out soon enough who I was driving with. I decide to head over to the stores tent and get a cooler ready for our trip to the PRT.

As I prepared the cooler of drinks and snacks I listened to the radio. The song that caught my attention was Hello Walls. It was my parents 'song. I can still picture Mom and Dad dancing to that song on their anniversary. I can't help but think about my family in Newfoundland. I long to be at my parents' cabin. It's funny, but when I was a child I didn't care to go to the cabin with my parents. Maybe it was because we were there almost every weekend or whenever Dad was off work. Or maybe it was because as I got older I wanted to be with my friends and party. But now, I find myself longing for what I once didn't want. I guess that's life. You don't know what you have until it's gone.

As I placed the cooler in the truck my co-driver came over and introduced himself. His name was Dan and he worked in clothing stores. By the expression on his face he was either very excited or nervous. I figured it would be in both of our best interests if I went over a few drills with him, just in case something did happen.

I had just met Dan, so I don't know how much he knows about our 'action on' drills. I had enough to worry about without worrying about some guy who does not know what to do if we get into any trouble outside the wire.

After a brief talk and a quick check of our truck, I checked the time and saw it was time for us to head to the convoy meeting area. Once there, the communications guy checked our radio and the convoy commander gave everyone a quick O group and we were on the road.

We made it as far as the main gate. Well, our front vehicle made it as far as the main gate and then we all came to a halt, not knowing what the problem was. After around forty minutes of sitting there, anger started to build inside me. Questions started running through my head. Why are we just sitting here? Is one of our vehicles broken down? Have the orders changed?

The more I thought about it the angrier I got. That is, up until I saw two soldiers carrying a young boy on a stretcher. The boy looked to be no more than twelve or thirteen. He was not moving much on the stretcher but I could tell he was alive.

His clothes were torn and I could see bloodstains on them. The clothes that weren't bloodstained were covered in dirt. As the stretcher passed by my truck I looked down and I could see that the boy had been beaten. His face was bruised and there was dried blood on his face and coming from his nose.

My co-driver told me what was going on. He was wearing the headset and he'd just heard it on the radio. The young boy had come to the front gate of the camp looking for medical help. Turns out he was raped by a group of Afghan men and left for dead.

I felt like the smallest person in the world. Here I was upset that we had to wait for a few minutes only to find out that this was why. This caused me to think about Avery and how I would feel if something like this happened to him.

How could a man do this to a young boy? I knew that Afghan men had 'man love Thursdays' when men had sex with other men. In this country they do not have sex with their women unless they plan to have a child. They do not use protection or understand what protection is. So to stop pregnancy they have 'man love Thursdays.' But what they did to this poor boy is terrible. The men who did this should have the same thing done to them.

* * *

For the next few days I stayed on the camp and did jobs around the compound. I worked on a few trucks, doing things like changing the oil or fixing a flat tire. Smaller jobs like that were left for us truckers to do. The maintainers were overworked enough; they didn't need the extra work of doing oil changes and changing a flat tire. The maintainers were so overworked they had to move to a twelve hour on, twelve hour off, shift. I always said when it comes to a field unit nobody works harder at the Service Battalion than the maintainers.

One day, I was lying on my bunk relaxing when Doc walked in.

Doc – Jamie, a new mission came down.

There was a pause, and by the look on his face I could tell he was about to give me some bad news.

Doc – And the warrant officer and the lieutenant think you're the best man for the job.

Another pause. This was starting to get on my nerves.

Jamie – Just tell me what you want me to do, Doc.

Doc – You and Mike will be attached to the artillery. You will join them to support the PPCLI (Princess Patricia's Canadian Light Infantry). The PPCLI are joining with the American Special Forces to take out a group of Taliban soldiers. You guys will be with the artillery to provide support for the attack.

Support? How could a trucker provide support? Unless I am driving a truck with rations and water in it. It has to be that. What else could it be? It's not like I would be driving a refuelled. That would be crazy.

Doc –You will be driving the refueler so you can keep all the vehicles in the battle refueled.

Jamie – The refueler? That's nuts! Has this ever been done before?

Doc – No, nobody has ever done this before. That's why we are talking to you about it. Drive a refueler carrying ten thousand litres of diesel oil to support a battle! I didn't want to do it, but I thought to myself, 'If I don't do it someone else will have to do it.'

All I could picture in my head was all the guys here with kids. I could not push the job over to one of them. What if something happened and they got killed? Then a kid would lose a parent. I figured that because I didn't have any kids it was best if it was me who was going on this mission.

Jamie – Okay, let's do it.

Usually when I agree to do a job for Doc, he would smile and shake his head or say something like 'Right on.' But this time he just shook his head.

Jamie – Have you told Mike yet?

Doc – No.

Jamie – Let me tell him.

Doc – Sure, go ahead. It will save me from telling him.

Jamie – No, you have to come with me to confirm it for him, because there is no way he is going to believe me. I just want to see his face.

Mike's face was priceless. I never saw his eyes open so fast in my life. When I told him what we were going to do he was lying on his bunk watching a chick movie, like he always liked to do. His eye opened wide and he jumped up from his bunk screaming, 'WHAT?'

Other guys nearby must have heard Mike because they started to poke their head through the tarp walls of his room to see what was going on. They were all as shocked as Mike to find out what we were about to do. Doc confirmed what I had said and then he left. The rest of the night we talked about this mission. Most of the guys thought it was crazy and a bad idea. Mike was like me. He was glad it was us instead of someone like Cody who has kids.

The next day Mike and I got our truck ready for our mission. Where better to start than at the mess hall where we had a good breakfast. I usually don't eat a big breakfast, but today I had a hunger on. It was the most I have ever eaten for breakfast.

When we got to the compound we went straight to work on the truck we would be driving on this crazy mission. It was a ten thousand litre diesel refuelled. It was just like a HLVW. The only difference was that the refueler was carrying a ten thousand litre tank of diesel fuel.

Our truck seemed to be in pretty good shape, as good as we were going to find. According to the orders we got from WO Baker, we would be leaving the camp at five in the morning. Because of that we thought we would get our cooler ready now. Might not have time in the morning.

After Mike and I checked everything we could think to check and we were happy with how the truck was operating, we drove it down to the sleeping area. When people had to be at a convoy as early as Mike and I, the WO allowed them to take their vehicles down to the sleeping area in order to save time.

After Mike and I got something to eat we headed over to the PPCLI tent to get our orders on what our role would be on this mission. When I walked into the large tent of the PPCLI, I had to take a minute and look around. If I had to describe it to someone I would compare it a circus tent. The floor was wooden pallets and bunk beds were lined up wall to wall inside the tent. There was no such thing as privacy here. It was like one big bedroom.

Mike and I walked through the tent, passing by soldiers of all ages and genders. Some were lying on their beds reading, some were writing, and many were playing games on laptops and Xboxes. I noticed a few of the soldiers were no more than nineteen or twenty. So young and so ready to fight for their country.

At the other end of the tent was a small meeting area that was set up for O groups, and that was where Mike and I went. We found out in full detail what we would be doing. A large group of Taliban had been seen in an area and the PPCLI, along with the JTF (Joint Task Force) and the American Special Forces, were going to fight and push this group of Taliban in to an area called the belly button. Our refuelled would be close to the belly button, along with the artillery. When the Taliban got to the belly button, the PPCLI would radio the artillery and they would bomb them.

The plan sounded fine. But the problem the PPCLI had been having was that the belly button was a long distance from the camp. That's where we came in. With the refuelled included in the mission they would have enough fuel to complete the mission. But who wants to drive a refueler into a mission like that? Who wants to be that close to the enemy while driving a fuel truck? Well, I can tell you who. Two guys from Newfoundland, that's who. Once Mike and I got our orders we headed back to our sleeping area.

That night I called both my parents and Vanessa. I didn't tell them about my mission. One, because I was not allowed to talk about our missions to our loved ones over the phone. That was in case someone was listening over the phone or our loved ones had loose lips. I also didn't tell them because I thought it was better if they didn't know for their own sakes. I didn't want to be the cause of their worry. I didn't want to be a burden. It was so good to hear all their voices. I even got to talk to Avery, and he sounded very excited to speak with me. He kept talking about things we would do when I got home.

After my phone calls were all done I headed down to where the truckers hung out in our sleeping area. I sat there until 9 p.m. talking with the boys. I figured I would not be seeing any of them for at least two weeks. At nine I headed for bed. I wanted to be well rested for my convoy.

At four in the morning I awoke to the sound of my watch alarm going off. Even though I didn't get much sleep last night, I was wide awake. I got dressed and headed outside to go and brush my teeth. Once I got outside I was met by Mike. He was fully dressed and just sitting at our table, smoking.

Jamie – What time did you get up?

Mike – I got tired of lying there looking at my watch so I got up. I might have got three hours sleep if I was lucky.

I left Mike to finish his smoke while I went to the bathroom to piss and brush my teeth. Within minutes we were both locked, loaded, and ready to go. We walked down to the truck and once we got there we had to decide who would be driving. Mike said he wanted to drive and since I really didn't care he climbed in behind the wheel. The truck engine ran while we loaded all our gear into the cab and behind the seats. With the gear loaded and the truck ready we were off to the convoy meeting area.

At the convoy meeting area there were so many people, mostly infantry soldiers getting their personal gear ready. Mike found our spot in the convoy and parked the truck. As soon as our engine was shut off the communications guy came up to set our radio so we both jumped out to have a smoke.

We hardly had time to light our cigarettes before we were called over to have our O group with the convoy commander. He didn't have anything to say that I didn't already know and the same went for Mike. So we stood there and used the time to finish our smokes. When the commander finished we headed back to our trucks. Mike and I put on our protective gear and climbed into our truck, Mike behind the wheel and me on the radio. I took along my video camera. Thought I would get a few videos to show my folks when I got home.

I heard a voice come on the radio asking for a confirmation from each vehicle. One by one the vehicles reported in. As the radio man for this vehicle I radioed in our call sign. I stared at the first vehicle, at its front tire, waiting for it to start to turn. Then it did turn and the front vehicle was in motion. We drove past the main gates and all the way into the city. Then past the city and into small village after small village. Then down through sand dunes where I could feel my heartbeat quicken because of the fear that we might get stuck.

I used to love getting stuck in the mud when I drove, but here it made me scared. We traveled over roads that had holes so big a car could fit in them. They must have been made by an old IED. There were times when it seemed like you were driving forever over a desert and then the next thing you knew you were driving through a village. One minute you think to yourself, 'There is nobody out here' and then the next minute you see a man standing all alone in the middle of nowhere. I could not help but think to myself, 'What is that guy doing there? Why is he just standing there?'

It was crazy at times when we had to drive on ground that was not level and our truck with its load of fuel was at an angle. I often thought our truck was going to tip over. But it never did. Mike drove that thing like a champ. Hour after hour passed and Mike continued to drive until the day turned into night. I wondered if we would ever make it there. Then word came on the radio that we would be stopping. We were now in the area where the artillery would break off from the rest of the convoy in order to set up. I guess this would be our home for the next little while.

There was not much to look at. To the east I could see a little house off in the distance. Close to the house I could see a goat, and to the west I could see a small mountain. North and south was just more desert. I was amazed that for hours we had driven through sand and desert and now I could see a house and all around the house is green grass and healthy trees. It was proof that not all of the country was destroyed by war. Some beauty was still left.

We parked our vehicles in a large circle or, as we call it in the military, an all around defence. Besides us there were two LAVs. That was our protection. Plus a Bison, even more protection. We also had two LUVWs with us. Captain Hilton, an artillery captain, was in one of those LUVWs.

When Mike shut off the engine I decided to head over to talk to Captain Hilton to see what he expects from us while we are here. He seemed nervous when I was talking to him. Maybe he was nervous because this was his first tour or maybe it was because he was in charge out here in enemy land.

After our talk, I learned that he only expected one thing from us and that was to give people fuel when they needed it. It sounds easy enough to me. I head back to our truck and tell Mike what our job will be and, just like me, he likes what he hears. Since it was late we set up our tent and went to sleep. There are soldiers manning C6 machine guns on each of the LAVs parked at our front and back. Hope the guys stay awake.

The next morning Mike and I wake up and come outside. I head around our truck and take a piss behind it and out of sight. As I am finishing up I hear Mike from the other side of the truck.

Mike – Holy crap! Oh yeah, you want some of this?

My first thought is that he is in trouble so I quickly run to his aid. When I get there I see Mike holding a shovel and trying to push a snake away. The snake is fighting back and biting the shovel. I stand back and watch as Mike battles the snake until it is far away from our truck. He came back to the truck still holding the shovel.

Mike – I moved the tent and there it was, just lying there. It must have crawled under our tent and used our body heat to keep itself warm.

The thought that I had slept with a snake last night made my skin crawl. After a ration pack breakfast we decided to walk around to each truck and see if they needed fuel. We walked from vehicle to vehicle with our protective gear on and our weapons in our hands. It turned out that everyone needed fuel. After that long convoy the trucks were thirsty. It took us about an hour to fill all the vehicles in our little circle. Then we parked back in our spot and filled our own tank. After that, we jumped in our truck and we both drank a bottle of water from the cooler and finished it off with a smoke.

We sat in the truck and talked for hours and then sat in silence. I guess after so long you run out of things to say. I had my DVD player with me but that was only good for one movie. We couldn't play music. We didn't even have a book to read. In all the preparation for this mission, we never thought to prepare for having nothing to do. Plus, because the vehicles never moved, there was no need for any more fuel.

Day after day we sat there with nothing to do but eat rations and smoke. The days seemed so long. I found a book of writing paper in one of my bags and decided to start writing. But what do I write? I was told once that you should write about what you feel. Well, sitting here in the quiet what I feel is alone. Even though I was sitting with one of my best friends, I felt alone. I felt far away from my family and the people who love me. I don't think. I just write. And here is what I wrote:

Lonesome Soldier

Lonesome is a word that stands alone
And lonely is how I am feeling today
Sitting here without a soul by me
Everyone I love so far away

Sitting here counting the hours until I return
Waiting out the days until I am home
Wishing I was somewhere else instead of here
Somewhere I won't feel so all alone

I think of your face smiling at me
With your arms open wide for my embrace
Showing tears of happiness that I have returned
Both of us knowing in your arms is my place

Seems like ten years since I felt your touch
Or the warmth of your body lying next to me
Falling asleep just so I can wake next to you
In your presence is where I dream to be

But then I open my eyes and you're no longer there
The loneliness returns as I'm back in this place
But I know I can close my eyes to see you again
Knowing that I can do that brings a smile to my face

* * *

One night, a few hours after supper, Mike climbs out of the cab of the truck and starts to look through one of the compartments on the outside of the truck. After a few minutes he climbs back inside and tells me that we don't have any poop bags. Poop bags were little bags that you tied to a portable toilet seat. Well, these things were not ordered for transport. We had none in stock. With no poop bags it means that Mike and I have to dig a hole and hover over it to do our business. So when the sun went down that night Mike and I ventured off with a shovel in hand. We got about three hundred meters from our refuelled. I dug a small hole and Mike dropped his pants and went about his business. But the problem Mike was having was the wiping. When we leave our trucks we have to be dressed in full protective gear and because Mike was a bigger guy like me he was having trouble wiping. I turned around and smiled to myself because there was no way I was going to try and help.

A few nights afterwards, it was Mike's turn on C6 watch and I decided I would sit up in the LAV with him. It wasn't like I had much else to do.

Since it was late at night Mike spent most of the time looking for the enemy through night vision goggles. I sat there smoking and listening to him talk. Mike kept going on and on about things he did when he was young and how much trouble he got into. Then for some reason he got quiet, but he was still looking through his night vision goggles. The first thing that popped into my head was that he had seen something.

Jamie – What is it?

Mike doesn't speak.

Jamie – Mike. What do you see?

A few more seconds pass then Mike takes off his glasses and looks at me.

Mike – You know the hot artillery chick?

Jamie – Yeah.

Mike – She just changed her clothes right in front of us.

Mike got to watch the whole show, her changing. She had to know there was someone up here manning the C6 machine gun and that someone would see her. None the less, Mike loved the whole thing.

The hours were like days to me, spending my time sitting in the cab of the truck and waiting. I called this a learning experience because now I know I need to start taking music or things to read with me. Mike and I had run out of things to say to each other.

One night at around 11 p.m. I was lying in the tent trying to get some sleep. Seeing it was 11, I knew Mike would soon be finished his turn on C6 watch and be heading back to the tent. I heard footsteps approaching.

Mike – Jamie, you'd better get up.

Jamie – Why? I've got my boots off and I am going to sleep.

Mike – You need to come out and see this.

I slowly sit up and put my boots back on and climbed out of the tent and stood next to Mike. When I got outside I could see why he wanted me to get up. About one kilometer away from our location there was a convoy of more than ten vehicles headed right for us. We both thought it would be a good idea to head over to the C6 again and see what is going on. When we got there we were met by Captain Hilton.

Mike – Hey sir, who are those people?

Capt Hilton – I just checked on the radio. We have no friendly in the area.

That meant the vehicles coming towards us could very well be the enemy.

Without a second thought Mike and I ran back to our truck and grabbed our protective gear and went back to the C6. By the time we got to the C6 there were other people getting their protective gear on. I looked up and I could see that the big artillery guns were changing their point of aim to the approaching convoy. I think to myself, 'This is it. I have been here two months and now I am about to be in my first fire fight.'

The artillery guns were locked on target. Everyone was locked and loaded, ready to fire. I could feel my heart pounding in my chest. All I could think about was how bad this was going to turn out. Just before Captain Hilton was about to give the order to fire I heard a voice come through his radio.

Voice from radio – Hello, this is Captain McClellan from C company. We are just passing through your area.

We lowered our weapons and stood there watching the artillery guns go back to their original position.

Mike – Well, I don't know about you, but I could use a smoke.

I agreed with Mike.

Just as well to go back to our truck and have a smoke. It's not like either of us could sleep now anyway.

For the next couple of days we kept seeing people off in the distance, and because we could not identify these people we would get a stand-to. A stand-to means we should be battle ready and take cover in our trucks.

We had a small group of the ANA with us and every time unknown persons or vehicles came close to us they would go out and chase the unknown persons or vehicles. The ANA worked very fast. Within seconds they would be aboard this little Chevy S10 and take off. If I was an Afghan person I would not want these guys after me. Canadians were easier on the Afghan people than they were.

The ANA didn't take any chances. They were rough, tough and to the point. If they felt any nearby danger they acted first and thought about it later. But over here that is the way it is. We could not shoot until fired upon but they didn't have the same rules of engagement as we did. As a matter of fact, I don't think they had any rules of engagement at all. But if I was raised over here and had to live my life over here I would act just like those brave ANA men. When you are raised in war it's hard to be lenient to anyone.

As the days went on I continued to find it very lonely. Even though Mike was sitting right next to me I felt alone. I kept thinking about my home or being at my parents' cabin. How I wished I could be standing next to the river right now with a fishing pole in my hand, hearing the sound of the water and feeling the cool breeze on my face. But that was not for me. I must sit day after day here in the cab of this truck watching the hours go by.

Mike goes for his daily C6 watch and I decide to write in my journal. When Mike returns he has a smile, something I have not seen on him in awhile.

Mike – Guess what? I just got word that they plan to send out replacements for us.

Jamie – No way! Don't play with me, Mike.

Finally, I am going to get out of here. I am sick of being here. One minute I am bored, the next minute my adrenaline is pumping like a mad man.

Mike and I couldn't wait for the day to be over. As soon as it was dark we headed to the tent to go to sleep. We were asleep for about two hours when the guy manning the C6 thought he saw someone in the distance. So they decide to fire off a par flare, something that is used to provide light over land so soldiers can see the enemy. Some are fired by soldiers, but this was the artillery so they used an artillery par flare. They shot it next to our tent and I awoke to a very large bang. A bang so loud that not only did it wake Mike and me it shook the ground we slept on.

My first reaction was shock. My second reaction was to jump out of the tent and grab my rifle because I thought we were under attack. When Mike and I climbed outside we realized we were not under attack and we found out what was going on. The two of us stood there with our rifles in our hands and breathing deeply. Before I could say anything, Mike had left my side and headed for the guy who just fired the flare. I won't tell you everything he said to the guy. But let's just say if that guy fires another one he will be sure to let Mike know.

That night, I had a nightmare. I was at my parents' cabin and I was sitting at a table and looking out a window. It was night time and I could see the headlights of vehicles coming in the cabin road. I watched as my father went outside to see who was approaching. But when he stepped outside he was shot in the chest. I heard Mom start to run. And then suddenly I was awake. I was alone in the tent. Mike was already up.

I climbed out of the tent and was greeted with a great surprise. Our replacements had showed up. This was finally our ticket out of here and back to the camp. Mike and I wasted no time in getting our truck ready. Plus the convoy was not sticking around for long. The only people being replaced were myself and Mike. Looks like someone thought it would be a good idea to switch up the fuel truck and get a full one out here. Whatever gets me out of here works for me.

Before we left we gave our replacements a quick assessment of what was going on and what would be expected of them. Once they were happy, we put on our protective gear and jumped in our truck. The trip back to the camp was a good one; our convoy wasn't touched.

That night after a good meal from the kitchen Mike and I decided to head down to the PX and buy ourselves some things to pass the time in case we get a tasking like our last one. I bought a MP3 player and a little speaker. That way, I can listen to music while I drive. I also bought some magazines and some boxed set TV shows. I figured a movie would be done in one night but a box set would do me a week. I was glad to have music in the truck with me again.

The next day it was great to be able to have a good breakfast at the mess again. I have learned to love those scrambled eggs with everything. I talked to some of the cooks who worked at the mess. Some of them were soldiers and others were civilians. They all loved cooking for us and they gave the soldiers whatever they asked for. Some of them even came out and said it was an honour to cook for the troops.

Once I got up to the transportation compound I didn't bother to walk into the driver's room. I thought there was no point and no doubt every phone is in use right now. I decided to head over to the stores tent for a bottle of water and a smoke. I figured the warrant officer would be out soon enough to give us a list of things to be done in the compound. God forbid the guys just sit around and relax for a morning.

At the tent there were a few of us sitting around enjoying a smoke and listening to the radio. It was good to have some time to talk to the boys. After being stuck in a truck for so long it was really good to see them again.

Dave was there, he just works on the camp now. I don't blame him. Every time he has been out on a convoy he has been hit. I don't know if I could handle going out again either. The doctors gave Dave some pills. Not sure what he is taking, but I do know he sure is a lot calmer.

We had time to have one smoke before the door to the dispatch tent opens and out walks WO Baker.

WO Baker – Task for you, boys. We need to get eighty-five jerry cans of diesel filled for a mission.

To the left of the stores tent sat the refueler; to the left of the refueler sat about one hundred empty jerry cans.

Doug said he would get the refueler going and I said I would find out what vehicle was going to be used and pull it up by the jerry cans. Before I took one step the WO shouted out the plate number of the truck being used. I quickly found that truck and parked it by the jerry cans. Without having to talk, the eight of us set to work. Two guys were in the back of the truck loading the cans. Two guys were working the hoses out of the back of the refueler and filling the cans and four guys were passing full cans up to the two loading. It was like we were being timed or we were in a race with some other men loading a truck. We were in a groove. Until the unexpected happened.

One of the guys working the hose was Colin and it looked like he was having some problems with the nozzle at the end of the hose. I walk over to see if I can give him a hand. But when I get over to him, he accidently knocks the nozzle off the end of the hose and the diesel comes out at full force and hits me in the chest. My first reaction was to spin around and then the diesel fuel is hitting me in the back.

Jamie – Turn it off. Turn it off!

Colin – I can't!

Colin turns the lever on the hose back and forth with no change in the force on the fuel coming out of the hose. Seeing this, Dan quickly jumps up into the truck and kills the engine. With that, the fuel stops and there I stood completely drenched in diesel. I stood there looking at Colin, but my sight was a little blurry because of the fumes coming off me.

Hearing the commotion, the WO came outside. We told him what was going on and he tossed me keys to one of the SUVs in the compound. He told me to go get a shower and change, and then exchange my clothes at clothing stores. I did just that, a nice long shower. The last thing I want is to get some kind of skin problem over here. The guy at clothing stores sure thought my story was funny.

When I got back to the compound it was close to quitting time. The boys were just finding out what they were doing tomorrow then loading up a bus that was being used on a tasking. As I was heading over to see my tasking for tomorrow, WO Baker came outside to meet with me. He pulled me aside and told me about my tasking. Tomorrow I would be attached to the PPCLI as their fuel driver. Jason would also go, but he would be driving a truck full of water and rations. As he was telling me this Jason walked by. The WO stopped him so he could tell him about our tasking.

Jason – Oh! So the three things the enemy needs most are food, water and fuel and we are going to carry it all while we are attached to the infantry? Well, that just sounds lovely.

I laugh at Jason's reaction. WO also told me I would not be driving one of the refuelers. I would be driving an HLVW filled with jerry cans of diesel. WO said because of the high level of danger in the areas we were going to this was the safest way to transport fuel. Plus, there was no chance of the fuel pump failing. I had to agree with what the WO was saying. The WO did have one good thing for us to share while we are out there. A satellite phone. At least while I am out there I will have a way to call my family.

Jamie – How long are we going to be out there?

WO Baker – As far as I know it's for two weeks. The convoy rolls out at seven.

Once the WO was finished talking to us, Jason and I jumped on the bus.

That night, Jason and I made sure we had a good meal at the kitchen since we would be on hard rations for the next two weeks. I also made sure I had music to go with me in my truck. Jason and I hung out with the rest of the guys that night. We would not be seeing them for awhile so it was almost like saying good bye to family. We have all become so close that you hate to see someone have to leave the camp for a long period of time.

That night I had another nightmare. This time Vanessa had been shot and I was holding her bloody body in my arms as I sat on the ground. Her skin was so white and her blood so red as her dead eyes looked up at me. But what grew inside of me was not sorrow, it was anger. Anger towards whoever did this. I didn't know who did it so my anger becomes focused on them all. They all must pay. And I am God's punishing hand.

I quickly sit up in my cot. My body is covered in sweat. I look at my watch and it's five minutes before my alarm is going to go off. Just as well to get up now. I get cleaned up and dressed, meet up with Jason and we grab a bite to eat. We get to the compound and we both load a cooler with goodies for each of our trucks. After we loaded our coolers our two co-drivers showed up. They seemed like cool guys. They were both infantry reserves and being that was my background, I didn't mind having them around.

With everything loaded we were off to meet up with the PPCLI. We didn't meet at the usual convoy meeting area. Since there were so many vehicles going out in the convoy we just linked up with them at their area of the camp. Since this was a combat mission, our convoy was loaded with LAVs and Bisons, all filled with infantry soldiers. We pulled up and parked at the end of the row of parked LAVs. We sat there watching these young men loading their magazines and prepping their gear. This is what soldiers call prep for battle.

By eight that morning our wheels were turning and we were out the main gate. Those wheels kept turning for the next thirty-six hours, only stopping for quick breaks along the way. Sometimes I thought it might be so people could take a piss and other times it was because our lead vehicle was not sure where to lead us. It wasn't their fault. They were doing a great job, but the land was just so rugged. Sometime we drove over places I thought for sure my truck was going to get stuck. But it didn't. It made it through even when we were driving through sand so soft I thought it was powder. It made it through all the washed out parts in the roads we traveled on. Even though it was weighed down with all those jerry cans, it made it through.

Once the night was over and the day had come back, people were getting tired. When drivers get tired the job becomes that more dangerous. Now the driver is not alert. The vehicle in front of me was an LUVW and I watched it roll over three times. Throughout the night we had to drive with night vision goggles. I hated that because half the time I could not see where I was going. It was easy for the guys who were driving vehicles with hatches. But inside one of those HLVWs it is near impossible to see.

At around two in the afternoon we finally moved into an all around defence. It was at this time I was told we would be stopping for food. I guessed this would also be the time that people would come and look for more fuel. The plan was, people would bring me empty jerry cans and I would replace them with full ones. Problem was, it was always a pain in the butt for me to have to tie down and cover the load. I would get the order we would be moving in five minutes so with that I would tie everything down and cover the load. Just as I finished, someone would come along looking for fuel. So I would have to uncover the load and undo the cargo straps and take out the full jerry cans. Then just as I got the load covered again someone else would come looking for fuel. It only took minutes but it was frustrating.

So that's how we spent our days, driving and stopping. Sometimes we would be stopped for hours on end. Sitting with our vehicles pulled in tight together. Just a way for us to get some cover in case we are attacked. We would sit there while the infantry did patrols around or checked out villages. Sometimes we had to spend many hours parked in the middle of the desert with nothing to do but talk to each other and wait for your turn on some watch. But when you're the guy with the fuel, you find that passing out the full jerry cans and taking back the empty ones becomes a full time job.

One day Jason climbed into the cab of my truck and told me about this group of Afghan men who have a couple of baseball gloves and a ball and they want to learn to play baseball.

Jamie – What will we use for a bat?

Jason – I have a handle from a pick outside. We can use that.

It sounded like a good plan, so why not. We used our interpreter to help us explain the basics. Then we set up the bases and home plate. I decided I would be the pitcher. Our glove supply was a little short, but our first basemen had a glove, our catcher had one and so did our center fielder.

The first batter, after two swings, made contact on the third pitch. But he only hit the ball on the ground to me so I quickly picked it up and tossed it to our first basemen. To my surprise, he actually caught it. Now when I told these people the rules of baseball I told them that the runner must be tagged with the ball to be out. Maybe this was not the best description because the next batter hit the ball to the second basemen and he then picked up the ball and didn't toss it to the first basemen. He decided to throw the ball directly at the runner. The throw was a good one. It hit the runner directly in the chest. Down the runner went with a thud. He lay on the ground in a cloud of dust.

The Afghan men who were watching cheered loudly and shouted, 'Out! Out! Out!'

With that, the game was on. It was a lot of fun and for one moment I stood and watched as some soldiers joined in with the Afghan men and they all soon were playing jokes and pushing each other in fun. It was good to see everyone enjoying each other's company. But after about an hour it was time for us to pack up and move to a new location so we had to call the game.

That night we drove through Kandahar city and the orders passed were that we would be driving without the use of our lights. We would be using our night vision goggles and that meant I could not see a thing while driving the HLVW. I was worried someone was going to jump in front of my truck and I would not have enough time to stop.

I could hear loud bangs outside our cab. The noise startled me and my co-driver. My first thought was that it was people shooting at us. But then something hit my windshield and I realized it was rocks. The people in the streets were tossing rocks at us as we drove through their city. I can't really blame them. After all, we are driving through their city with no lights on. Rock after rock hit my truck as we passed through the city. At 12 a.m. we held up for the night in a small compound that was being run by the ANA. We were told to go to ground and at 5 a.m. we would be moving in to a new position where Taliban had been seen. The news came as no shock to anyone, it was the same news we got every night. Move to a new location and in the morning the PPCLI would do their searches for the Taliban. I truly believe that the medals worn by the PPCLI are not big enough. These men were heroes. I have often seen movie stars on TV and watched how people cheer for them. People should be cheering for the Canadian light infantry because they are the true heroes.

I didn't get much sleep that night because I had constant visits from soldiers with empty jerry cans. It's not like I could say "Sorry, I need sleep.' These guys needed fuel so what can you do?

The next day we were on our way. Once near the designated location the vehicles Jason and I and a few others were driving were held up and the infantry moved in to where Taliban soldiers had been spotted.

Sitting here with our vehicles pulled in tight together, I decided it was a good time for me to get something to eat. So I pop out a ration and try something new. I place my ration on the roof of my truck to see if it will actually cook there. I leave my ration there, grab my rifle, and walk away for a smoke. I figure smoking next to my truck is not the best idea so I walk over to Jason's truck and join him. He was already smoking and talking to the interpreter.

Jamie – What's going on?

Jason – This guy has been bugging me since we left the camp to put on a movie. He said he has never seen a movie before and would like us to show him one.

So this guy has never seen a movie before and it was up to us to show him his first. What movie should we play? Then it came to me and when I told Jason he quickly agreed with me. The movie we played for that man that night was the vampire movie *Blade*. We thought it would be funny to see this guy's reaction to a vampire. We popped the movie into a little portable DVD player and let it play. Everything seemed to be going fine. He was very quiet while the movie played and seemed to be enjoying it. Up until the vampires came out and blood started falling from the ceiling and you could see people popping out with sharp vampire teeth. That's when our interrupter began to freak out. He started talking really fast in his own language and then he started loudly asking us what was wrong with these people. After I settled him down I told him that these people were vampires and I described what vampires were. Then he looked me straight in the face.

Interpreter – Oh yes, we have vampires in Afghanistan.

I quickly paused the movie and looked him straight in the face.

Jamie – What do you mean, you have vampires in Afghanistan?

Then he proceeded to tell me about a small village not far from where we were where there was a hill with a cave and in the cave lived a large man who only came out at night and when he came out he killed and drank the blood of sheep and goats.

I think to myself, 'I don't think that guy is a vampire but it does sound like he's a problem for the people in the village.' So I ask the interpreter why someone doesn't take care of the guy. He told me the people in this village have attacked this guy. He has been stabbed and shot many times, but he still attacks the animals at night. I had the interpreter show me on a map where this village was. That way I will be sure to avoid it.

That night I thought about calling home, maybe to check on how Vanessa is doing. Or maybe to let Mom know I am okay. It has been a long time since I called either of them. It's not that I don't want to talk to them; I just find it hard to listen to them. I miss home very much and listening to them makes me miss them and home even more. Plus, I don't know what to talk to them about. It's not like I can talk to them about what's going on with my day. So I can only listen to what they say which brings me back to my first problem. I sit there with the phone in my hand, but I do not make a call.

The next morning we were on the road again at the crack of dawn. Well, I guess you can't really call it a road since we were mostly driving across country. We drove through some massive dried out river beds. I remember spending hours driving along cliffs looking for a way down to where what little remains of the river. At one point we had to drive down over a very steep mud hill. It was so steep that the back four wheels came off the ground. All that was touching ground was my front two wheels. Then I brought up in a mound of dirt, sand and crushed rock at the bottom. I cut the wheel hard to the right and finally settled at the bottom. But that was the easy part. The hard part was trying to climb out and up the other side.

After we got up the other side we drove for another hour until we got to a place where I felt nervous driving. It was a narrow road with what looks to me to be some kind of sand pit on one side and a high wall of rock on the other. To me, it looked like a good place for an ambush. I could see the other end of the sand pit. It looked to be just over one kilometer long.

Word came through on the radio to keep the vehicles tight together and try and make it through the area as fast as possible. Everything was going great until after five hundred meters the road turned into a hill. As I slowed, I geared down. My vehicle slowed down. The spacing between my vehicle and the one in front of me was getting bigger and bigger. I geared down again but I could not keep up to the vehicle in front of me. Something seemed wrong to me. My truck should not be going this slow. I check my gauges and everything looks good. I look out my mirror and that's when I see I have a flat tire. It was my center tire. I turned to tell my co-driver about our bad luck but before I could speak he said something to me.

Co-driver-- We have a flat tire on my side. It's the center tire.

I get him to radio to the lead vehicle about our problem. The only thing we can do is change the tires in this bad area. I get out of the truck and run next to the flat tires. I am greeted by a young lieutenant. He asks me how long this will take and I tell him an hour. He sets up an all around defence with a few other vehicles around my truck. I look back at Jason's truck and I see he is already taking off his spare tire. Each of our trucks carries only one tire. I will need them both.

By the time I have the first tire off Jason is by my side with his spare. He put down his tire and tried to help me take off mine. Because of its size and weight it was a two man job to get the tire off. For some people it would be a three man job. When we went to remove the tire Jason noticed something. The tire had a small hole in it. It looked like a bullet hole.

Jason – Two of your tires were blown out at the same time and this one has a hole like that. I think someone shot out your tires.

That thought in our head turned out to be great motivator because Jason and I set to work knowing we had to get the tires on and get back on the move as fast as possible. After we got the first tire on, the lieutenant returned for a status update. I told him about the hole in the tire. I could see that did not sit well with him. After the second tire was on I looked at my watch. Thirty-five minutes. That's got to be some kind of record. We have never been able to do it that fast before. With the tires replaced we were back on the road. We drove until midnight, and then we moved into a tight formation and got a few hours sleep.

We were all told not to sleep under our vehicles, the reason for that being because a while ago a soldier decided to catch a few hours sleep under his vehicle and throughout the night the vehicle sank into the soft sand and he was trapped underneath and suffocated. I set up a cot next to the front tire of my truck and while I was doing that the satellite phone rang. It made me think about the people I loved in Canada. It brought my mind back to Vanessa. I wondered how she was doing and if she thought about me as much as I thought about her. Part of me wanted to call her and hear her voice again, but for some reason I couldn't. For whatever the reason, another night passed by and I didn't call home.

Five hours later we were up and on the road again. We drove for about another four hours until we stopped again and moved our vehicles into a tight formation, a Léger. We were stopping so we could get some food into our stomachs. I decided I would eat my food outside the cab of my truck. Even though it was very hot outside I thought anything would be better than spending more time in the cab.

A LAV was on the left side of my truck and a few soldiers were sitting there eating rations. I talked to them, trying to get to know the people I was working with. In talking to them I discovered that the PPCLI soldiers have given me the nickname Fireball. They thought I was either very brave or very dumb to be driving a truck carrying so much fuel. It was good to know that the people I thought were the bravest people I have ever met thought that I was either brave or stupid. My answer to that could be summed up in four words: a little of both. As we were talking a sergeant came over to join us.

Sgt. – The lieutenant doesn't like the look of that wall over there.

The sergeant pointed at a wall over to the left of our formation. The wall was made of mud and rock and stood about fifteen feet tall and was about a kilometer long.

Sgt. – He wants us to blow a hole in the wall so we can see what's on the other side.

Two of the guys get up from their lunch and grab an 84mm cannon from the back of the LAV. They move into a safe location from us and fire the cannon twice and make a large hole in the wall. When the dust settled we could see through the hole, and what we saw was what looked to be a small village. I could see what looked to be mud huts, the same kind of huts we've seen Afghan people living in here in the mountains.

The guys placed the cannon back in the back of the LAV and continued to eat their rations. The sergeant stuck around and sat on the LAV with the rest of the boys. When my food was gone I turned to head back to my truck, but before I turned away one of the guys invited me up on the LAV to join them for a smoke. I agreed and quickly climbed up and pulled out my smokes. The sergeant tossed me a lighter and I lit up. As the sergeant tossed me the lighter he saw something.

There was a man looking at us through the hole in the mud wall. The sergeant quickly brought this to our attention and at the same time we all snapped our heads towards the hole. But when we looked, the man was gone.

Sgt. – Wait for it. Someone was just there.

We keep staring at the hole in the wall and sure enough the sergeant was right. We watched as a man's head slowly peeked out at us and then he left. A few minutes later he peeked out again and left. But this time it looked like he had something in his hand. With Taliban having been seen in this area we had no choice but to consider this a threat.

Sgt. – Have your rifles ready.

The Afghan man stuck out his head again and looked over at us.

I watched as the sergeant got down off the LAV, slung his rifle over his shoulder, and started walking toward the guy in the hole in the wall. Then one of our guys got down on his stomach and put his point of aim on the hold. The other guy got up and manned the 50-calibre machine gun.

The sergeant didn't get very far before the man in the hole pulled out an AK-47 and shot at us. I watched the rounds he shot make splashes in the mud around us. But as quickly as they started, the rounds stopped. The soldier lying on his stomach with his rifle quickly returned fire with a single shot.

I watched as that one bullet hit the Afghan man in the head and the air turned to red mist.

The PPCLI are well trained, and that sniper with the rifle just saved our lives.

* * *

As the days passed we have driven through so many villages and dangerous areas where Taliban have been reportedly seen that I have lost count. Through these days I have found my opinion changing about these people who call Afghanistan their home.

When I first stepped off that plane all I wanted to do was help these people. But now, after seeing what they do to each other with the rape and the abuse, I find my patience for them has disappeared. These people no longer looked like people to me. Now, they looked like animals.

My mind felt torn, one part of me hoping to never have to pull the trigger of my rifle. But there was another part of me, the darkness in me that wanted to pull the trigger, that wanted nothing more than to have these people feel my wrath. I could feel this darkness growing inside of me like it was trying to take over. When the darkness first comes on I tend to space out. The reason for this is because I picture in my head everything that I want to do to someone when I am controlled by the darkness.

I picture an Afghan man coming up to me. He is looking for something, like they always do. They never come to you to talk or to offer you anything. They just want something from you all the time and I am sick of having to give up smokes every time I see one of these guys. These people would be your friend to your face and as soon as you turn around they would shoot you in the back for a buck.

I picture this man standing in front of me. He starts screaming at me because I don't understand his language. Once the man starts to raise his voice I can feel the fire burning inside of me. It's like a ball of energy trying to explode out of my body. Unable to hold it in, I lose control and grab the man. I pick him up and slam him onto the rocky ground. As soon as he hits the ground I am on top of him and I am punching him in the face until his face is a bloody mess. I can picture the whole scene in my head and it's so real and detailed.

Jason – Jamie. Hey, man, you alright?

Jamie – Yeah, man. I'm okay.

Jamie – Cool. Let's get ready. We are headed to Camp Wilson.

We quickly pack up our stuff and are on the road to Camp Wilson. On the way there we have to drive through a place called 'Ambush Alley.' I've never liked the place because of that name.

Before getting to Camp Wilson, we had to make it to the highway. I had no idea at the time but it took us six hours to get to the highway. Six hours of driving across country where there were very little roads. A lot of times we would be following a brook, driving on it like it was a road. When we did this, we would always meet Afghan people at every stop. I guess when the people found water they stayed next to the water. There were places we stopped where you would never think people would be living.

One day the convoy stops and we are all now parked in the middle of a brook about fifteen feet wide. To the left of my vehicle was a small hill surrounded by trees. After about ten minutes, word of a long halt comes over the radio. I shut off my tuck and open my door. I light a smoke and relax for a second. But when I turned to look up at the hill it was like I watched it come alive. People started to come out of the hill like they were living in caves or something. Many of them were children from ages five to thirteen. They all came up to our trucks with no fear. They were scratching the palm of one hand with the other hand. I remembered this was a sign of them asking for food. I have always had a soft spot for kids, and when I looked at one of the boys it was like I could see Vanessa's son Avery looking up at me, asking me to spare him some food.

I got back inside my cab and closed the door. A soldier has to think about his life first. What if one of those kids has a gun or a grenade and wants nothing more than to end my life?

But then I took some food and some of my rations and threw it all out my door and closed it again. I watched as the kids ran for the food, grabbing for what they could. I grinned as I watched them eat their treats and was happy to see them smile. I remember a young boy and an even younger girl sharing a candy. He would suck on it for a little then pass it to her to suck on for a little while. Like a brother and sister.

But then I watched as some older kids came and took what they wanted from the younger ones, and took it with force. I watched how they hit and punched each other for the candy. I then realized I should not have done what I did with the food. If I choose to give anyone any more food it will be from my hand to their hand.

Word came back to us that Alpha Company was in a battle with some Taliban. So far it's been one Canadian soldier killed and about thirty Taliban killed. That would explain why we were stopped for so long. Turns out our convoy was waiting to get orders from headquarters on whether or not we were going to make our way to the battle to help Alpha Company.

Moments later the word came that we would not be needed because Bravo Company was closer and they would move in to help and we were soon on our way again. We drove on for about another hour and then the vehicle in front of me decided to stop. The vehicle was a small pickup truck completely filled with the ANA. They all jumped from the back of the truck and ran off to the left and up to a small mud hut. This made me nervous because the more time this truck sat still the further the other vehicles traveled away from us. If there was one thing that scared me out here it was getting separated from the rest of the other vehicles. A few minutes later the ANA soldiers came running back to the pickup carrying a goat over their heads. They jumped back into the truck and we were moving again.

We had been driving for hours when the convoy got an order to stop. It was mostly for a bathroom break, and for truckers like me it was a chance to check our load. I slowly climbed out of the cab of my truck and jumped to the ground. The soft powder like sand fluffed up around me in a cloud and I could not help but feel a little like Pig-Pen in the Charlie Brown cartoon I remembered watching when I was a kid.

Once on the ground I began to slowly walk around my truck to see if everything was still secure. The load seemed to be fine and all my cargo straps were still nice and tight. After I finished my walk around I thought this would be a good time to have a smoke. So I pulled my pack out of my pocket and then searched for my lighter. I felt it in my pocket and reached my hand inside to pull it out. But when I pulled it out I didn't have a good grip on it and it dropped to the ground and bounced under my truck. I let out an annoyed moan at the sight of my lighter bouncing under my truck because now I knew I had to get down on all fours and crawl underneath to look for the stupid lighter.

I got down on my hands and knees and took a look under the truck to locate the lighter before I started to crawl underneath. When I looked under I found more than just a lighter! Right next to my lighter I noticed two strands of wire that were next to each other and sticking out of the ground. In Canada this might mean nothing but here in

Afghanistan with all the buried mines, I didn't want to take any chances.

I passed word of what I had found on to the officer in charge. He agreed with me: you can't take any chances over here. Once he saw the wires he decided it would be for the best if we had our bomb squad check it out. These guys were who you called when you found an unexploded improvised explosive device or a bomb.

Once the bomb squad was on the scene the first thing they told me to do was to slowly back my truck up and away from the two wires. I climbed back in my truck and started the engine and watched as everyone moved into a safe location. This did not make me feel any better. I placed the truck in reverse and slowly moved my truck back. I moved the truck about twenty metres back from the wires. The bomb squad set to work to see if they were actually attached to something.

I watched those guys dig around the area and slowly expose what was underneath the wires. After almost two hours of slow digging the bomb squad found the wires were attached to a five hundred pound bomb. The fuse for the bomb was the two wires that were sticking out of the ground. If a vehicle tire had driven over the wires, causing them to touch, then the bomb would go off.

Thoughts started going through my head. What if I was driving just inches to the left? I would have driven right over those two wires. There is no way I would have survived the blast from a five hundred pound bomb under my truck. Scary stuff.

We carry on for another few hours before we hit a problem. One of our LUVWs breaks down and the decision is made to use my truck to tow it. We decide to place some Afghan soldiers in the vehicle being towed. The vehicles were hooked together, not with rope or chains, but with something more secure. We used a large A-shaped steel bar. This would make the vehicle behind me have no choice but to travel as fast as me and also exactly where I drive.

After the first hour of driving the convoy stopped and I jumped out to go back and check on the Afghan soldiers in the truck I was towing. The truck was completely covered with sand. I could not see in through the glass window. I opened the door and all I could see were piles of dirt and sets of eyes staring out at me. Most people might be a little nervous in their position, but these people looked more than happy to be there. For the next four hours I checked on them every hour and each time they seemed to be in good spirits. After four hours we end up at Camp Wilson.

Jason and I parked our trucks off to one side at Camp Wilson. I was feeling hungry so I decided to take out a ration and toss it onto the roof of my truck. I knew that the heat from the sun on the roof would cook my food for me.

The infantry soldiers were pushing hard through villages and towns and were pretty tired so I suspected we would be here for at least a day. Jason and I set up our cots outside in what little shade we could find and sat back and enjoyed a warm Coke.

Camp Wilson had not changed much since the last time I was here. It's still a large square piece of land surrounded by a brick wall with two-storey towers at two corners which are manned with C6 7.63mm machine guns. Last time I was here there were Canadian soldiers manning the guns. Today, there were ANA soldiers manning one of the guns.

Our platoon kept one guy at Camp Wilson to man a refueler at all times. Jason and I decided to go see who was manning it. We found it was Larry, another young guy from Nova Scotia. He was one of those guys who came to Afghanistan a little overweight and he likes to talk about the weight he has lost while on tour. When we arrived at his truck he was sitting on a lawn chair underneath a large tarp he had set up to shade him from the hot sun. It was a pretty sweet set-up and I knew if I had to man the truck here in Camp Wilson I would be doing the same as Larry. Larry also had his DVD player going and was watching a movie. Jason and I decided to join him. It was good to see Larry. Funny how when you are away from the rest of your platoon you come to miss them and worry about how they are doing.

After some small talk Larry pulled out something that I once took for granted. Cold drinks! Larry had just started manning the truck so his cooler still had ice in it. Jason and I smiled at each other as we both opened a can of ice cold Coke and begin to take a long drink. It was so cold that it burned going down the back of my throat. Usually I would stop because of the burning, but it tasted so good I just could not stop. After our drinks we sat on either side of Larry and joined him in watching his movie. About twenty minutes into the movie I could hear people arguing in the watch tower we were sitting next to. It was the three Afghan soldiers who were manning the machine gun in the tower. Their arguing turned into a slap fight, almost like what you would see if two drunken women were fighting. This soon got the attention of everyone at Camp Wilson.

Suddenly one of the Afghan soldiers jumped back from the other two and picked up an AK-47. He cocked the weapon and pointed it at the other two men. He then began to shout some words at the men as they lifted up their hands. All was quiet in the camp as we looked to see what would happen next. Then a voice was heard from the distance, from one of the PPCLI soldiers.

"Do it, you pussy!"

The camp broke out into laughter.

The ANA soldier lowered his weapon and the boys and I finished watching our movie. That night before I went to sleep I thought it would be a good time to call back home to Canada and check in on Vanessa. It seemed like the longer I went without phoning home the harder it was to call. When Vanessa picks up the phone and hears me say hello she screams my name. She is so happy to hear my voice. I thought she might be mad at me or yell at me for not calling in such a long time. But she wasn't mad at all or at least she hid it well. I didn't say much, I just wanted to listen. I could close my eyes and it felt like I was sitting there on the couch listening to her tell me about her day. Back then I mostly pretended to listen to her talk but this time I really wanted to hear everything. I decided to sit up in the refuelled and talk there. Why walk over to my truck when there was one right here? By the time I got up into the cab of the refuelled and sat down behind the wheel Vanessa was on her third story. She kept talking and I just sat back and looked up at the stars.

When I woke up this morning in Camp Wilson I noticed a small water pump running over by the water well. I was not really sure what the water in the well was used for, but I know it was being used for something and this pump should not be there. It wasn't long before the master warrant officer (MWO) of the camp heard about the water pump and ordered some soldiers to get rid of it. So three soldiers took the water pump with the hoses and threw them outside the main gate of Camp Wilson. The rest of the day I carried on with my work and at night I went to sleep. The next day there was the water pump back pumping out water again. So again three soldiers were ordered to get rid of it. This time they got some hammers and beat the pump up before getting rid of it. The next day the pump was back again. This continued all week long. Every day some soldiers would beat up the pump and each morning the pump would be back. The pump would be held together with rope, glue and tape but it was still running. You have to say one thing about the Afghan people. They can sure fix things.

After two days at Camp Wilson we headed out into the countryside again. Our convoy went over terrain that most people would only attempt on horseback. We stopped at village after village, checking out any place that Taliban had been seen. It seemed like every second day the infantry boys were in a fire fight. Some of these boys were not old enough to legally buy a beer in Canada, but here they were fighting for Canada.

Each village we visited would have its rape victim, or men who beat women. I could not understand why you would hit a woman or a child. And with rape, a lot of times it would not be just one person raped by another, it would be a gang rape, and the gang rape could even happen to a child. Seeing kids get hurt was the worst thing for me. My anger grew and grew towards these people and how they could treat each other this way. It came to the point that I no longer wanted to help them. I wanted them to pay. I wanted everyone to pay for the harm they had caused.

After two months of driving from village to village, we finally got the order that we were heading back to camp in the morning. I was very excited about that order. I could not wait to get a cooked meal from the kitchen and a hot shower. It's going to be good to see the boys again too. I have grown so close to these men that I consider them family. I miss them the same way I would miss any of my family members, so hearing that I would be getting back to my brothers was music to my ears.

The next day at about 10 a.m. I could tell we were getting close to the camp because we were driving through

Kandahar city. The vehicle in front of me was a LAV and whenever we came to a speed bump it would shoot ahead of me because I had to slow my vehicle in order to drive over the speed bumps. I didn't like having space between us. The last thing I want is a vehicle getting in between us. So once I was over the speed bumps I hurried to catch the LAV. I was up to about 80 kph when a woman dressed in black suddenly stops out on the highway in front of me. My first reaction is to turn the wheel and try to bypass her but do I have the time? Do I take the chance and maybe hit the wall? Or do I just drive over her? For that one brief second I think to myself, 'Just run her over, Jamie, you can say there was nothing you could do.' At the last second I turned the wheel and missed her by inches. I think to myself again, 'Maybe it's time to go home.'

We arrived back at camp and it was good to see the boys. That night, I called Vanessa. When I got her on the line she spent most of the time talking and I spent the time listening to her. She told me how Avery misses me and how he has been asking for me and wanting to know when I would be home. Hearing that gave me mixed feelings. I still don't know if I am ready to be called Dad or if I am ready to settle down. Ever since I've been in the military all I've thought about is my career; I wanted to go everywhere. But I am smart enough to know that when you become a father your whole world changes.

I worry about being a father. Being overseas has changed me, has made me a very angry person. I don't want to be a father if I am going to be angry my whole life. I don't want to be one of those fathers who beats their kids or is never there for their kids. Maybe Vanessa and Avery would be better off without me. Maybe Vanessa will forget about me and meet some guy who will treat her and Avery right.

After about an hour of listening to Vanessa, I decided to call Mom and Dad and see how they were doing. Just like Vanessa, they were very excited to hear my voice. My mother said she watched CNN news all the time to see if any Canadians were killed that day. She said she always held her breath until the name of the soldier was released. Mom told me how people dropped by the house all the time to ask her how I am doing and to make sure to pass on to me that they are praying for my safe return. It felt good to know that my whole hometown was behind me. Mom also told me she wanted to send me a package and asked if there was anything I wanted or needed. I said socks and underwear are something you can never have too much of over here.

Once my phone calls were done I headed back to the truckers' sleeping area and checked to see what I was doing tomorrow. It was a nice change to see that I would be working in the transportation compound. It was great sitting back and talking to the boys and hearing about what their days had been like since I last saw them. Seems like everyone over here in the trucker world has a story.

Today on my convoy I have a trucker for a co-driver. He is one of the master corporals who will be taking over for us when we head home. The guys replacing us are mostly posted in Petawawa, Ontario.

We will be making a run to Camp Wilson. We had to drive a refueler there to refill the one that is already there. My co-driver didn't seem nervous about going off the camp for the first time. He seemed more eager to learn the way things are run here and what it's actually like off the camp. We chatted a bit. I told him what to expect from the ANA and the Afghan people. Everything was going smoothly and we were getting close to Camp Wilson; we just had to drive through Ambush Alley.

We were on the last long stretch before we hit Camp Wilson when all of a sudden I felt my truck shake and then drop down on the passenger side. I saw a burning tire roll past us. Then my co-driver heard a message on the radio, but even before he spoke I could tell by the look in his eyes that we had been hit by something. He said that according to the driver of the vehicle behind us we were hit by a RPG (rocket propelled grenade) on the back passenger side tire. The blast knocked off the tire and that's why I had seen it roll past our truck.

We then came under fire; I could hear bullets ricochet off the truck.

Co-driver – They are telling us not to stop.

Jamie – Don't you worry. I have no intention of stopping.

Even though we had lost a tire I pressed down on the gas and drove that truck as though I had stolen it. The axel was dragging along the pavement; sparks were shooting out the back of the truck.

When we got in view of the camp the shooting stopped. I pulled into the camp and everyone there was on a stand-to. I parked the truck inside the camp walls and quickly jumped out for a smoke. I thought I could use it. As I sucked back on the cancer stick I walked around the vehicle to have a look at the damage. The tire was completely blown off and there was some fire damage, but the fire was out.

Some people came up to me to see if I was okay and I said I was fine. They told me they'd heard the RPG hit my truck and went on stand-to. One officer walked up to me and said it was a good thing I was carrying water. When I corrected him and said I was carrying 10,000 litres of diesel they left me standing alone with my truck.

I don't know how many smokes I had while I looked at that truck but I know it was a good many. While I was having one of my smokes, I was told to grab a bite to eat because in thirty minutes I would be taking another refueler back the same way I'd come, though Ambush Alley. Since my truck was no longer driveable I would be leaving it here and driving the one I was going to refuel back to the main camp.

On the way back it seemed the convoy moved a lot faster, which was just fine with me. The drive back went smoothly and we arrived safe and sound. On the camp, the boys asked me if I was okay and I said I was. I went to my bed and sat there. I looked down at my hands and I could see them shaking: My rock hard nerves were no longer rock hard.

* * *

Today was a good day at the camp. Today was the day the singers were coming. I'd heard that Canadian country music star Julian Austin was one of the singers flying in. That was cool news to me because I was a fan of Julian and really hoped to meet him. The singers were going to be here for the week so I thought in that time I should get a chance to meet him.

Day one, I had no luck meeting him because the singers spent the day with the higher ranking officers. Day two, I was busy down on the runway so I didn't get a chance to meet him then either.

On the third day, I was put on a convoy but it was a short one, just to the PRT. I figure forty minutes out and forty minutes back plus maybe an hour there so maybe I will be back in time for lunch. My co-driver was not a trucker, but someone on their first trip outside the wire. He didn't say much, spoke only when I asked him a question or made a comment. I figure since he didn't want to talk much I would just turn on my MP3 player and listen to some music.

When we arrived at the PRT I quickly parked and unloaded my truck. Once the truck was unloaded I parked back into formation with the other vehicles of the convoy and waited. While I was sitting there listening to some music the camp was rocket attacked. The rocket was not that close to me but it was close enough. Within seconds the alarm was sounded and people were racing for cover. I put on my helmet and sat in my truck.

Within minutes a group of infantry were tasked out to try and find or capture who was attacking us. The first thing in my mind was, 'Now I have to wait here even longer.' I guess most people would be more worried that the enemy would shoot at us again. But when you have a job like mine you get used to being in these situations. Nothing against the other trades here, but if there are two trades that seem to become numb to the attacks it is infantry and truckers.

In about thirty minutes the infantry force came back and they had a prisoner. It was just one man. Our orders are to turn all prisoners over to the ANA so that's what was done. The man was turned over to the ANA and they placed him inside a small wooden shack. But he wasn't placed in there alone. He was followed in by some ANA soldiers. I didn't think too much of it at the time. Just figured it must be guards keeping an eye on him.

* * *

By the fourth day of Julian Austin being on the camp I was starting to lose faith that I would get a chance to meet him. But then luck came my way. I heard that the singers would be doing a tour of the camp today. So that meant they would be stopping by the transport compound. That was good news for me because I was working in the compound today. Standing in the supply tent having a smoke and a bottle of water I watched in excitement as the bus entered the compound. The bus stopped and one by one the singers stepped off. Then I watched Julian step off the bus. There he was. GI Jules. I wanted to meet him not just because I liked his music, but because I know he tries to do so much for the men and women in the armed forces. I also know how much he works with the Wounded Warrior's fund. (Julian Austin did a tribute song called *The Red and White Brigade* in order to raise money for the Sapper Mike McTeague Wounded Warriors fund).

I didn't want to be one of those guys who runs up to a famous person and acts all crazy so I just stayed back and watched for a bit. I watched as the boys all got to shake hands with Michelle Wright and The Wilkinsons. Meeting those singers gave everyone a minute to forget where they were. I finally walked up and shook Julian's hand and introduced myself. I knew to make him remember me I had to do something to help him remember. Julian was videotaping everything and everyone he met. Luckily, I had my camera with me so I began videotaping him as he was videotaping me. Then I decided to act like Grover in Sesame Street and play the near/far game. I ran up to Julian and said 'Near' and then I ran away and said 'Far' and I kept doing this over and over until everyone, including Julian, was laughing. That night the singers came to Canada House to sign autographs and meet with all of the soldiers. Julian thought the best thing to do was take out his guitar and start a sing-a-long with the soldiers. So there he sat with his guitar and within seconds he had soldiers singing along with every song he played. I videotaped everything. Before too long Julian was joined by the other singers and everyone was singing together, it was a magical moment, it made the soldiers feel like they were home.

The next day I was on camp refueling with Dan. There weren't too many stops on the list so we knew it would be a short day. When we were almost finished we decided to stop in at Canada House for a drink and a smoke. When we got there I was pleasantly surprised to see Julian standing there having a smoke. When I stepped up onto the patio he turned around and saw me.

Julian – Hey Jamie, what's happening, my brother?

I could not believe he remembered me.

Jamie – I'm doing camp refueling today. What are you doing?

Julian – Oh, I've got a meeting, but what I want to do is go visit the people in the hospital. I have nothing against high ranking officers, but I want to meet the troops.

It felt good to hear him say that, so I thought how about I take him on camp refueling with me.

Jamie –Want to help me refuel the camp?

Julian looked at me with a surprised look on his face.

Julian –Are you serious?

Jamie – Oh yes, let's go.

I told Dan what was going on and within minutes Julian and I were off finishing off the few stops I had left on my list. As we worked together we talked a lot about his father and his family and I spoke of my family. We spoke about our love for our family and our country and for some reason I found it very easy to talk to Julian. Funny, I find it hard to talk to my family but it's easy to talk to this stranger. After we made our last stop I drove over to the hospital so Julian could visit with the injured soldiers. He was inside for about an hour, but I didn't mind waiting. When he came out I drove him back to Canada House. I asked him if I could email him from time to time and he seemed excited to give me his email address. Then we shook hands and he climbed out of the truck. That night was the first show the singers were doing and what a show they pulled off. The soldiers had a blast; the only thing that was missing was the beer. The next day the camp was on a bit of a stand down, giving soldiers and the singers the freedom to relax.

That night was the second show. Mike pulled out a bottle of rum so some of us got to have a few drinks. It didn't take too much and I was feeling the booze and eager to see the second show the singers were going to do for us.

About halfway through the show word came down that a convoy had been hit and a female captain had been killed. She was the first female of the tour to be killed. The convoy was held up at Camp Wilson and needed a resupply and a pick up for the wounded. So for us that meant a truck had to be loaded ASAP. A trucker ran through the crowd yelling 'MOVE' and 'CLEAR A PATH.' Us truckers ran to the compound and started to load one truck with food and water and another one with fuel. Brad and John were selected to be the drivers. As soon as the trucks were loaded a quick hug and the words 'Love you, man, be safe' were spoken by all then into the trucks and off they went driving into the darkness.

* * *

The next day, it was mid-afternoon and I was hanging out in the supply tent listening to some music. There was this old country song playing on the radio, it reminded me of the cabin, hearing Dad playing his old Gibson guitar and singing away.

The WO came out with some news for us about a convoy that was out. They didn't get hit by the enemy but something went wrong. Turns out that this convoy did not even make it as far as Kandahar city before they hit a lot of traffic. The convoy headed down the highway through Kandahar city just like any other convoy, down the center of the road. This caused the rest of the traffic to have to pull off to the side of the road. That made one Afghan man angry and he decided to drive back onto the highway. When he did this he had a head on collision with an LUVW. Riding in the LUVW were three soldiers. One was driving, one was in the passenger seat working the radio, and one was in the turret of the vehicle. Not all LUVWs had turrets but the ones that did definitely looked cool.

When the Afghan man drove back onto the highway and hit the LUVW in a head on collision, it killed the soldier in the passenger seat instantly. The guy in the turret had ducked down inside the cab, which was normal when driving through a city. His body flew forward and his helmet brought up in the turret causing the helmet to tear off his scalp. His body kept going forward through the windshield. The only ones to survive were the two drivers. When the medics made it to the side of the young man who went through the windshield, he could not speak. There was no hair or skin on the top of his head. All he could do was blink. The young man was flown to a hospital in Germany.

It's getting close to ten at night and the boys still in camp were around the sleeping area all having a bottle of water and exchanging stories. But tonight the stories were not about things that happened over here in Afghanistan or even about what happened while on other such missions. Tonight the boys were talking about what they wanted to do the first night they got back home.

The first thing everyone agreed on was that a trip to the beer store was in order. I think that's something that goes without saying for most soldiers. Even if you don't drink, a trip over here will make you want to drink.

Guys with children wanted nothing more than to hold their kids again. I didn't have kids so I could only imagine how hard it must be to be away from their kids for such a long time. Not only is it hard on them but it must be hard for the children as well. For me, all I wanted was to be at my parents' cabin and have Vanessa by my side.

While we sat there the camp was once again hit by rockets. The first rocket did not hit too close to us. But the next rocket was in between some of the tents where there were large light poles with powerful lights on them for soldiers to see at night. Our sergeant was the first to see the rocket coming towards us. When he saw it coming our way he quickly jumped up and knocked the men who were standing to the ground. The rest of us hit the ground and waited for the blast to hit. But before the rocket reached us it hit a light pole about fifty metres from us and was deflected away out onto the street going to the PX. The rocket hit the road and exploded. We all slowly stood up, some of us not knowing what had just happened and how lucky we were to be alive. Just shows that all luck over here is not bad.

After being on the camp for a few days it was time for me to head off the camp again. Today I was doing a resupply to a camp called Gumbad. I hear it's a bad spot and what I hear must be true because they need to be re-supplied quite a lot.

On the way out we have to drive through a dried up river bed, something I had really learned to hate because there were just so many twists and turns. The reason I didn't like all the turns was because I didn't like not being able to see too far ahead of where I was driving.

As we were driving along, we come to a spot where the river bed road came on a huge slant. All the other vehicles were driving through very slowly and just barely making it without tipping over. That made me nervous because those vehicles were not carrying the kind of load I was. I was so scared that my truck was going to tip over. But what could I do? It's not like I could turn around. So very slowly I drove through this slanted area and I watched as my co-driver seemed to get lower and lower in his seat than I was. At one point the truck got so slanted I had trouble holding onto the steering wheel.

Then it happened! I could not see it but it was like I could feel the tires on my side lift off the ground and we started to tip. But as fast as I felt the truck start to tip I felt it stop. It was like something grabbed onto the truck and stopped it from tipping over. My truck had three wheels on each side and for this moment it felt like only three were touching the ground. I kept driving for a few metres and then my truck dropped back down on my side and we leveled out and drove on through.

After that we drove on for a few more hours until we came upon a spot where we had to drive up and out of the river bed. The problem was that the only place for us to go was up a slanted rock. Going up this rock did not look safe to me; it was at maybe a seventy degree angle and it was smooth. It would be very easy for me to drive up the rock but then the tires would lose traction and the truck would slide off to the right and crash down into the river bed. That was a fall I knew my co-driver and I would not survive.

Slowly my truck edged forward and I watched as one by one the other vehicles drove up the slanted rock. The LAVs and the Bisons had no problem. The LUVWs tires slid a little but they made it up. Now it was my turn. From the bottom, I could tell it was about fifty metres to the top, then a left turn to get onto the flat ground. I got the best run off I could get with the distance I had to work with and then I headed up the rock. For three-quarters of the way my truck made it up with no problem. But when I got close to the top my front tires started to slide to the right and come dangerously close to the edge. I cut the wheel to the left, but the truck kept sliding. I hit the brake. Now the passenger side front tire was hanging out over the edge.

I could hear my co-driver gasping as his side hung over the edge. Very slowly I put the truck in reverse and backed it up and managed to get fully back on the rock again. I kept the truck still for a second and without moving it I cut the wheel to the left and put the truck in first gear and slowly climbed the rock all the way up and onto the flat ground. When we arrived at Gumbad, the driver of the vehicle that had been behind me came running up to me.

Driver – Man, that was crazy back there at that slanted area.

Jamie – I don't know how I didn't tip over.

Driver – Man, you would have, but your truck hit a tree.

I didn't understand what he meant.

Driver – Your truck tipped to the right and it would have tipped over but it brought up on a big tree that sat on the river bank. Your truck was up against the tree and the truck kept sliding along the tree as it moved. When the truck came to the end of the tree that's where the slanted road leveled out and you flopped back down on four wheels.

I couldn't believe my luck. Thanks to a tree, I didn't tip over!

Not long afterwards my truck was unloaded and I was taking a well deserved break. As I stood there leaning against the large front tire of my truck I started to look around at Camp Gumbad. It was a very small camp, barely enough room to park four HLVWs. This camp didn't have the same protection as other camps. It had only a small barbed wire fence surrounding it and a large mud fort that the Afghan people had made. The infantry soldiers guarding the camp had made some changes to the mud fort to make it battle ready.

It was normal to see Afghan people walk up to the outside of the barbed wire fence and stand there begging for food or water. We were told not to give the people anything out of fear of starting a riot, but most of us gave what we could to the kids. Kids were my weakness. Every time I saw someone with a kid or a baby I would think about Vanessa and Avery or my little nieces and I would always try and help.

As I finished my smoke I noticed this older Afghan man walk up carrying what looked to be a baby. He was walking just outside the barbed wire fence and he seemed to be begging for food. Seeing him, all I could think about was this poor starving baby. I had to give him some food for the baby. I didn't think about whether it was right or wrong. I just thought that a starving kid isn't right.

I pulled two bottles of water and some food from the cab of my truck and walked out to the fence to meet the man.

He met me with a big smile on his face. But I wasn't ready for what happened next. As I passed the man the food and water for the first time I could really see the baby he was carrying. Even though the baby's eyes were closed I could tell it was no longer alive. The baby's skin had turned almost blue and there were flies on the baby's face. When I saw that, I was filled with anger. How could a man walk around with a dead baby trying to get food? What kind of country was this? Every part of me wanted to grab this man and pull him across the barbed wire fence and beat him until he was as dead as the baby he was carrying. Without even thinking, I raised my rifle to my shoulder and pointed it directly in the man's face. My finger was on the trigger. I could feel the stiffness in the trigger as I was so close to pulling. I wanted the man dead. I didn't care about anything else. I just wanted him dead.

I've said before that when I started this tour I wanted to help the Afghan people, but now I find myself looking at it a different way. I want the people who do the bad in this country to pay the price for what they have done. The darkness I could feel growing inside of me, the darkness I had never felt before, was taking over. I looked into the man's eyes and he looked back at me in fear. Seeing him frightened gave me a feeling of relief, a feeling of satisfaction.

Jamie – Get back from the fence or I will put you down!

The man didn't understand English so he just stood there. My fingers were still gripped around the trigger. And then I heard a voice behind me.

Jason – Jamie, you okay, buddy?

I could hear Jason's voice and I slowly let go of the trigger and lowered my rifle. The Afghan man turned and ran off. He was still carrying the baby.

We were all ready to leave when the sergeant was approached by a lieutenant in our convoy. He tells the sergeant that Taliban had been seen not far from here. The lieutenant wanted us to pretend our vehicles were stopped because they were broken down. He figured that way the Taliban would attack us. Once that happened the rest of the convoy would come in and kill the Taliban that were attacking us. When I heard the plan, I lost it.

Jamie – Sir, that sounds like you want us to be the bait.

Lt. – Well, no, Corporal. We think this plan will work.

Jamie – Call it want you want, sir. We are bait.

Even though I hated the plan I sat there for an hour, lying on my stomach in an all around defence around our vehicles waiting for someone to shoot at me so someone can come save me. Ridiculous!

That night I had another nightmare. It was about that same guy with the dead baby who I had seen at Gumbad. But this time he was in a mud hut and he had many babies and they were all dead. Then I looked down at my hands and they were covered in blood. I fell to my knees and began to cry. I felt like it was my fault. I try to wipe the blood from my hands but it won't go away. I keep wiping, over and over again, but still my hands are stained. Then came a huge explosion. I woke up. The explosion was not a dream. It was a rocket attack. This time the rocket landed around two hundred metres away from my bunk.

Scott – Man, that was close. You could actually hear the rocket cut through the air.

Jamie – I am so sick of this place.

Scott – Me too. I can't wait to go home.

* * *

Today I find out that I am heading back to Martello for a while. I'm once again doing the refueling thing. It's me and Brad going together this time. I don't mind that at all. I enjoy Brad's company. So I pack my truck with stuff I think I will need out there, some junk food and my music. Once my truck is ready I head back to my bunk area. I give a call home, but once again I don't talk much. I don't really want to talk to anyone back home anymore, it has become somewhat of a chore. I mostly do it for them so they will know I am alive. I hear Vanessa's voice but I'm not really listening. The same goes for my parents. I don't want to hear what I am missing back home. I just want to get this job done over here and leave this place.

That night I am hit with another nightmare. This time someone has kidnapped Vanessa and I am looking for her. I am in an apartment building and I know she is trapped in one of the apartments. I kick down door after door but I have no luck in finding her. I search and search until I wake up.

In the morning, Brad and I grab our bags and head for our truck. By the time we got our truck to the meeting area it was like everyone else was there waiting for us. Would not surprise me that we received the wrong timings but this was something I didn't care about anymore. We get our brief and are quickly in our vehicles and on the road.

We are about thirty minutes away from Camp Martello when the air conditioner dies. Within seconds the temperature in the cab is unbearable. With no windows to roll down and no way to get any air we had no choice to open the doors of our vehicle. But this is no easy task when you are trying to drive the vehicle. My co-driver could keep the door open the whole time but I could only keep the door open for a few seconds at a time since the transmission was manual and I needed both arms to change gears as well as steer. Even though we only had a short distance to go it seemed like it took us forever to get to the camp.

For weeks, Brad and I worked as a fuel station. Groups of infantry would load up in LAVs and go out on missions looking for Taliban. When they returned they would come to us to get topped up. At the same time there were a lot of soldiers driving the heavy equipment vehicles and building a protective wall around Camp Martello. They were also expanding the camp. Camp Martello has really grown since the start of my tour. First it was just an area of land with a wire fence around it. Now it had a large wall, computers with internet, a place for vehicles to get repaired so they don't have to be towed all the way back to the main camp. It was amazing how much it had grown.

I find myself getting less and less sleep now. The nightmares are just too much. Every night I seem to have one and they are mostly about the people I love back home.

For weeks now Brad and I have been in this camp. We have not seen any other soldiers we know. It makes you feel pretty alone in the world.

Brad and I made ourselves a bunker with a tarp over the top for a roof. We had our boxes of rations stacked up to block the wind from blowing sand inside. Getting sand in your sleeping bag sucked.

For a whole month we sat there waiting for someone to pull up needing fuel. That made for long days. I had a portable DVD player, but where do I plug it in? It's not like I have a generator. I've got one movie and my battery is dead.

Had to check my boots every morning there for camel spiders. I hate those things. They are huge compared to the spiders in Canada. We get rocket attacked here, just like in the main camp. I decide to volunteer to man the guns on the LAV at night. Gave me something to do, plus sometimes I think I want someone to attack the camp so I can shoot them.

After a month of being out here with Brad eating rations and with no shower it was finally time for us to head back to the main camp. I was excited to be heading back. I could not wait to have a shower. We were joining an infantry group that was also heading back to the camp. The morale was high in the convoy going back to the camp. Seemed like everyone in the convoy had been away from the main camp for too long.

The ride back was going well until one of our vehicles hit an IED. The LAV in front of me stopped and a soldier decided to get out and try and help the people in the damaged vehicle. Brad and I watched him jump from the front of the LAV and onto the ground below.

To everyone's surprise and shock he jumped right onto a mine and blew both of his legs off. Before the medic or anyone could get to him he was dead.

The people in the damaged vehicle were quickly taken out and loaded into the back of the LAV. Like I said before, every convoy has a vehicle called a wrecker in it and that is like a giant tow truck. The wrecker was hooked onto the damaged truck and our convoy was on the road again.

When we got back to camp we had an O group. In the O group we were told that during our tour more than four hundred Afghan soldiers had been killed. Numbers like that would make any man's blood run cold!

It was around five in the evening and a few of us had just finished eating at the mess and were headed back to the sleeping area. On the way back we passed by the gym where Americans were playing some ball hockey. Jason and I decided to stay and watch for a while. We might have been there twenty minutes when we were approached by one of the players. The first thing he asked us if we were Canadian and we quickly responded with a "Yes." He then asked if we could get a Canadian team together so we all could play Canada vs. USA in a ball hockey game.

Both Jason and I thought that was a great idea, so we told him to give us thirty minutes to get some people together and we would return. It took less than thirty minutes to find enough people to make a team; it seemed like every Canadian I asked wanted to be on the team. Around twenty minutes later we showed up with Team Canada all ready and rearing to go.

We were a close group of friends and this wasn't the first time we'd played ball hockey together. We soon discovered that it wasn't the first time Team USA had played together either. There was no referee and both team used that to their advantage by playing a rough game. There was no fighting but both teams played a rough game.

After the first period we were down two to nothing, and we were a little worried that we might lose this game. We were talking about our game plan for the next period and drinking water when WO Baker showed up carrying a large Canadian flag. He had it tied to a broom handle and was waving it around. But he wasn't alone; our Officer was there along with many other Canadians, all there to cheer us on.

By the end of the second period we had taken the lead 3-2. It was just like being at a gold medal game. The crowd watching would cheer for every close call or goal. Plus after the end of the second period, more Americans showed up to cheer on their boys. By the time we were into the third period it was like the United Nations, with so many people from so many countries watching and cheering us on.

We were getting close to the end of the third period; the score was tied 3-3. Both teams were having close calls but no one could put the ball in the net. By this time, even though the sun was going down it seemed just as hot as it was at noon. But it didn't affect anyone's pace; both teams were still putting their everything into winning this game.

With only minutes left the camp was suddenly hit with a rocket attack. The thunderous sound of the rockets hitting the camp put a halt to the game. Both teams had players drop to the ground on their faces; others took off running to find shelter in a bunker. We truckers had become used to getting fired upon so when the camp came under rocket attacks we didn't run for cover like other people; we just stood there waiting for the rockets to stop.

But Jason had other plans. He saw the rockets as his chance to win the game. With people lying on the ground and others running for cover, Jason runs down the court with the hockey ball and with a wrist shot put the hockey ball into Team USA's net.

Jason – Canada Wins!!! Canada Wins!!!

When the rocket attack was over, the Americans argued the fact that we cheated. But we all laughed at what Jason had done and we claimed the game a win for Canada.

* * *

One day, a few of us were hanging out in the supply tent when the Afghan cleaners came in. You could watch the mood in the men change as they watched the Afghans climb out of their small car with their brooms. The soldiers, including me, didn't like the Afghan people anymore. It was hard for us to tell who the good ones were and who the bad ones were. So we always had to have our guard up. Being this tense for so long can't be good for anyone.

The days seem longer now that I am not sleeping. And who in the world could sleep with all these nightmares? Seems like every day I am greeted with death. Either it happens to me or I hear about it happening to someone else. And when I sleep I am greeted with horrible nightmares of loved ones dying or being kidnapped.

Tonight I awake from my nightmare only to find out that we are being rocket attacked. The rocket hit a sleeping area somewhere on the camp and six people were hurt in the blast. It's things like that make it hard to differentiate between what is real and what is a nightmare.

* * *

Today we had to all meet at the supply tent in the transport compound. Nobody had any idea why we were being asked to meet there. And we really had no idea what was going on when we saw WO Baker standing there holding the same Canadian flag he had been holding during our ball hockey game.

Once we were all assembled, WO Baker told us that we had received a message from the Edmonton Oilers telling us that the team wished us the best and they were behind us. Then they asked that we all sign this flag because it would be sent back to Edmonton and hung in the Oilers dressing room. The team wanted the flag there to bring them good luck through the playoffs.

I am not saying that the flag gave them any luck, but I was told that before every game each player touched the flag on their way to the ice. That season, the Oilers made it all the way to game seven in the Stanley Cup Finals.

* * *

It's the fourth of July and I am on a ramp ceremony for two Americans who were killed when a chopper crashed. I have been to too many of these for my liking. Actually, one is too many for my liking. These soldiers are just like me. It could have just as well been me in that box with a Canada flag draped over it. I wonder would they give a flag to Mom and to Vanessa. I wonder who would come to my funeral. I salute the caskets as they pass by me.

WO Baker came to me today. He asked me if I was good to go. I hated when he asked me that because it meant one thing. He needed me to go on another long and dangerous convoy. I was right. I was going back out with Charlie Company. I didn't know if I had the nerve left to go back on a mission like that. After being out with the PPCLI for a month and a half already, I knew I would see more action. But being the person I am I could not say no. I kept thinking about who would have to go in my place if I didn't go. So once again I said 'yes' and packed my bags for another run with the infantry.

I had the same co-driver as when I was out with the infantry the last time. It was nice to see a familiar face. This guy was an infantry reserve, but he'd proved to be a good co-driver last time so I was glad to have him with me.

When I got to O group the night before our convoy was leaving I found out that this was primarily a rescue mission. The British had a camp around a five hour drive across country and they were under attack by the Taliban. Word had it there were about four hundred Taliban in the area. In the last two days, the British had lost seven men.

On the convoy to the British camp one of our HLVWs was hit by a rocket. But the rocket went through the driver's side window and into the cab of the truck. Once inside, the rocket ricocheted all around and then smashed out the other window. When I talked to the driver he didn't know what to be happier about, the fact that the Taliban have crappy weapons or that Canada has crappy windows.

Driving was scary. There was one time where we were driving on a narrow road and each side dropped off like a cliff down around five hundred meters. The drop off point was so close to the tires that my co-driver and I had to open our doors to keep an eye on just how close they were. It was the most terrified I have ever been. It got even worse when we had to drive at night and I had to use night vision goggles. In my vehicle, the night vision goggles were useless. Now I was not only driving next to cliffs but I was doing it blindfolded. A few times I went off the path a little, and once I had two of my front tires hanging off the side of the cliff before I managed to stop and reverse back onto the beaten path.

It was the night before our big attack and we were told to go to ground and get some sleep because we would be leaving before sunrise. I took out my sleeping bag and climbed out of my truck. For a second, I thought about sleeping under my truck but I remembered the story about a guy who slept under his vehicle and through the night the vehicle sunk into the sand and he suffocated. I decided to sleep on top of my truck, on my load, in fact. I was carrying food and water so I thought boxes of water would make a good bed. As I lay there I became very cold. I guess being high in the mountains of Afghanistan the temperature can drop some. I wrapped myself up in a blue tarp trying to keep warm and get a few hours shut-eye.

The next day we were off and moving before the sun was up. The British joining us in the fight were set up in the hills above the camp with mortars. The plan was for them to fire mortars onto a certain area to clear a path and then we would drive into the camp and resupply them and get out as fast as we could.

The fire fight went on for six hours. It was like the Taliban just kept coming. Then for some reason at 7 p.m. everything stopped. It was like everyone decided to take a five minute break. But when that five minutes was up it started again. The Americans sent in choppers that dropped two 500 pound bombs. I felt the ground shake when they exploded and I watched as a mushroom shaped cloud appeared in the distance.

When the dust settled we were given the word to head in. Just seconds after the word was given our tires were rolling and I was once again driving my truck as fast as if I had stolen it. With bullets flying by we quickly pulled into the camp and in record time we had everything unloaded.

Without even saying goodbye or good luck we headed out of the camp and back to where the Brits were set up with the mortars. I don't know how many Taliban were killed that day. I can just say it was a lot. The ANA had joined us on this fight and one of three men got shot in the neck, but he was still alive.

With the resupply over we joined back up with the British and were soon in a convoy back to our main camp. It was a long drive after a battle like that, but we all just wanted to get back.

On the way back one of our vehicles was hit by a rocket fired by a Taliban soldier. This hit was a little different than most. This time, the rocket did not explode. The rocket hit the vehicle in the driver's side door and not only stuck in the door but also stuck in the driver's leg. Even though the driver was in great pain he was able to pull the vehicle over and stop. His co-driver radioed for help and the driver was placed in the medic Bison. A new driver was put in his place so the convoy could carry on back to camp.

We were driving across country and there wasn't much of a road to travel on. We drove through dried up river beds and past small villages. Most times, you didn't know it was a village until you were alongside it or actually in it. My guess was a lot of people didn't want to be seen and they did a good job of keeping hidden. Many of the villages we passed had small vegetable gardens where the people tried to grow whatever they could. Most places I saw in Afghanistan the ground was no good for growing anything because it was mostly sand. But there were a few places that had green grass and trees growing. I didn't pay much attention to these small farms when we passed. I was too busy watching the road and my surroundings to care about that. With Afghanistan being so heavily mined I was very uneasy about us not being on a road.

Everything seemed to be going well until our convoy made a strange turn onto one of these farms that we were passing. Only thing was that this was no little farm. This was a big one that ranged about two kilometers in length. The plants growing on this piece of land were very tall; I am guessing about seven feet in height because they were hitting the windshield of my HLVW. Once we were through this farm land we broke out onto a dirt road and moved our vehicles into an all around defence. The word came back on the radio that it was going to be a long halt which meant that I had time to get out and check my load.

As I was checking the back of my truck one of the platoon officers walked up to me.

Lt. – What did you think of that?

Jamie – What's that, sir?

Lt. – Did you notice what we just drove through?

Jamie – You mean that farm land? Yeah, that was pretty tall plants.

Lt. – That was a marijuana field we just drove through.

Jamie – WHAT! But that field was like two kilometers long, sir.

Lt. – That's right.

I stood there in shock because I could not believe what had just happened. It was like something right out of a movie. When I got back to camp I didn't say much to anyone. I just headed for a shower then lay down on my bunk. I stayed in my bunk until 9 p.m. when another rocket attack occurred. This time it was very close to me. I actually felt the ground shake. I started to feel like I was living in a movie, like death was following me.

I am feeling on edge, every pop, every loud bang, and I jump. I get nervous in a crowd now because when I see a crowd it looks like a good place for a suicide bomber to hit, so I try and stay away from crowds. My sleeping is now an hour here and there when I can get it. Hard to sleep when you never know if a rocket is going to hit you. It's the Afghan people's fault I am like this. I hate them for what they have turned me into. I hate them all.

* * *

I spent the next few days in the camp doing work on vehicles and on my own personal kit. I liked cleaning my rifle, it relaxed me. Plus, it was good to keep your rifle clean. The last thing you want is your rifle to jam on you when you needed it.

Working at transport was getting harder and harder. We were losing people because our tour was coming to an end and people were being shipped back home to Canada. I would be one of the last to leave because I volunteered to stay longer. The reason I decided to stay longer was because I was unmarried and had no children. I thought it would be the right thing to do to let the married men or men with children go home first.

Even though I was staying longer it didn't mean I wasn't in a rush to get home. Just like everyone else on this tour I longed to be home with my loved ones. I couldn't wait to sit on my couch and watch some television, to order a pizza, or to go to the fridge and get a beer. Oh, how wonderful a beer is going to taste! I realize now how many little things I have taken for granted.

With the work done for the day I check to see what I am doing tomorrow and find out I will be riding in the back of a Bison. This is different for me. I am used to being the driver of any vehicle I am in. But this time it won't be me behind the wheel. Maybe it will be a nice change.

That night, I had a dream that Mom and Dad's house was hit with poison gas. I was in a truck and driving down the Trans Canada Highway in Newfoundland trying to get to their house before it was too late. I hate these nightmares. I never make it to the people I am trying to save.

* * *

Today the convoy I was in was headed out to recover two LAVs that had been hit by an IED. Adam and Larry were in the tractor trailer and I was in the security Bison. Our officer decided to join us in the Bison. He even wanted to man the C6 machine gun that was mounted on the Bison. On the drive there everything went smoothly. We can only pray nothing goes wrong when we try and load the damaged vehicle.

When we got to the site there were security vehicles manning both ends of the road and soldiers were dismounted and providing protection. The two LAVs were near a small village but still on the main paved road. We pulled up to the damaged vehicles and right away started to work on getting them loaded onto the trailer. To load these vehicles we pull up in front or behind and winch them onto the trailer. Then we chain them down and hit the road back to camp.

The tractor trailer pulled up behind the damaged LAVs and the boys started to work. The Bison I was in pulled up beside the tractor trailer to provide more protection to the boys loading the LAVs. Adam and I got out of the Bison to help in any way we could. But once a vehicle is being winched onto a trailer there isn't much else to help with. There's just a guy working the controls of the winch. As Dan worked the winch, Adam, Larry, and I stood on the side of the trailer and kept an eye out. At the same time our officer was in the Bison manning the C6.

A few kids from the village next to us decided to come up and see what we were doing. We gave the kids some water and what food we had. Adam was even playing catch with a little girl. He would lightly toss a small rock to her and she would giggle and toss it back to him. It was so good to see Afghan kids laughing and enjoying themselves. Having fun with these kids made me think of Avery. I can't wait to see him and see if he has changed since I last saw him. This moment with the kids almost made me forget about this horrible place I was in.

Off in the distance a small white car had pulled up onto the road and was facing us. The car caught the eye of our officer and he told us to keep an eye on it. Within seconds of him saying that the driver of the car pressed down hard on the gas pedal and came right at us. Our officer quickly fired a few shots at the driver of the car and the shots must have hit him because the car began to slow down. But when the car came to a complete stop, it exploded. The blast blew Adam, Larry and me into the air and we all landed close to each other. We were knocked out from the blast. I sat up, but I was not sure where I was. I was in a daze and I just sat there, a little dumbfounded by what had just happened.

I noticed Larry on the ground knocked out, and I saw Adam on his feet, but just standing there like he was lost. Adam had blood on him so I knew I should get to him to see if he was okay. But when I stood up I saw there was blood on me too. I started to check myself over to see if I was injured but I couldn't find anything wrong. I stood up and took a step towards Adam to check on him and that's when I saw something on the ground.

I was stepping on a child's arm. I stared at it in shock and horror for a minute. It was like what I was seeing was not registering in my brain. I looked at Adam again and this time I took notice of everything. We were both standing in children's body parts and blood. The suicide bomber had killed all the Afghan children who had been playing with us. That is why I was covered in blood, because of the children; it was their blood that was all over me. I walked over to Adam and could hear crunching under my feet with every step. I knew it was body parts I was stepping on. When I got to Adam he seemed to be okay. Just in shock like everyone else.

When we both came to our senses we headed over to Larry who was now waking up. We got Larry up on his feet and we all climbed into the back of the Bison. Our officer was pretty shaken up as well. He had taken some shrapnel to his face but at least he was alive. After that, we stayed in the back of the Bison until both the damaged vehicles were loaded and we were back in camp.

We went to the camp hospital and I walked from room to room checking on Adam, Larry and the officer to see that they were being looked after. I might have been there for an hour when WO Baker showed up and told me I had to leave. They needed me to go back out on another convoy that night.

Go out on another convoy? I thought to myself. After what I just went through? I looked down at my watch to see what time it was. But when I did, I didn't notice the time. I just noticed the shaking in my hand. Could my nerves handle going out again? Or am I on the verge of losing control?

I close my eyes and try to gather my thoughts. I have to get a grip on the task at hand. I know that if I say 'No' to WO Baker someone else will have to take my place. What if that someone has kids and doesn't make it home?

I open my eyes and tell him I am good to go. Better for me to go than someone's dad.

As I walked back to my sleeping area I could feel the hate towards these Afghan people grow more and more. How could someone do this to their own people? What is wrong with these people? They would kill their own people, their own children, just to try and take a few of us out. It's sick!

* * *

And now I had to go back out on another convoy. Does anyone know what I have just been through? But what with people returning to Canada and those who have been hurt our numbers are short. Plus we have some people who just can't take another trip off this camp; they are under too much stress from being over here. We also have those who are too afraid to go off camp anymore. Because of all of that, others have to pick up the slack.

The convoy WO Baker wanted me to go on was a trip to the PRT. It would be a short trip out and back. I really didn't want to go off the camp anymore. I just felt too burned out. But all I could think about was someone else having to do the convoy for me. I can't push my work off on someone else.

We had no problems on the way out to the PRT, but we were not so lucky on the way back to camp. To the front of my vehicle there was an LUVW and it was hit by an IED. When the LUVW hit the IED it quickly burst into flames. I watched as one by one the soldiers jumped from the burning vehicle and ran for cover. Finally, they were all out except for one. He was trapped inside because he could not get free from his seat belt.

There were a few rifles inside the vehicle, left behind in the panic to get out. People tried to rush to the rescue of the soldier in the vehicle, but the bullets in the rifles started to shoot off from the heat of the fire so nobody could get near the truck. We had to lie in the dirt and wait for the rounds to finish going off. By the time we could get to the soldier it was too late.

When I got back to camp a lot of the boys were at the transportation compound waiting for me. They'd heard what happened on my convoy and they wanted to see if I was okay. They asked me if I was alright and I didn't know what to say. Physically, I am fine. But I found myself not being able to think straight. All I could hear was that man screaming as he burnt to death. I could not get the sound of his screams out of my head. It reminded me of the Afghan who had been caught at the PRT and how he screamed before he died. For me, it was not the sights that got to me, it was the sounds.

For the next three days I felt like a zombie. It was like I didn't know or care what was going on around me. It seemed like everywhere I looked all I saw was someone in pain or someone doing something wrong. I could no longer see the good in people. All I saw was the bad. I wanted the bad people to pay for the wrong they had done. I could not let things go. It was like things that normally didn't make me mad were now making my blood boil.

I wanted to call home, but I didn't. My reason for not calling was because if I did I knew I would only bring someone down. I thought that if people heard the tone in my voice and the way I was talking they would see that I was not doing well over here and I needed to come home.

There is now only one week left to my tour. I am so close to going home. There are only a few of us truckers left. Most of the truckers here now are from the Canadian Forces Base in Petawawa. They are the guys who are taking over for us. Truckers like me who are very close to going home don't want to go off the camp anymore. It would be a shame to lose our life when we're so close to going home.

* * *

Camp Wilson needed someone to work the fuel station out there. WO Baker didn't want to ask me but I knew he wanted me to go. I thought it might be a good way to close out my tour. Spend the last week out there and then it's done. So I agreed to go out on this one last mission.

My week in Camp Wilson was going well. I was pretty relaxed there and I was not that busy. I had a book with me so I decided to give it a read. Within three days I had the book read. It was called 'Angels & Demons' and I loved it.

I was so tired of dealing with the Afghan people. Just listening to them talk makes me mad. That was a problem because I was the fuel man so whenever anyone needed fuel, including any Afghan men who were working with us, they came to me. Some days I would have just as many Afghan men coming to me looking for fuel as I would soldiers.

One day I was laying on my cot doing some light reading when I heard someone walk up to me. I heard a noise, a noise that someone would make if they were calling a cat. I looked up to see an Afghan man standing there looking down at me. I sat up on my cot and asked him what he wanted even though I knew what he wanted. He pointed to his truck that was parked out at the back of my truck and made that cat calling sound again. Without saying a word, I climbed up into the cab of my truck and started the engine. I then got out and walked to the back of the truck and started to fuel his vehicle. The nozzle on the hose was too big to fit into the truck and I had to pump slowly so as not to spill too much fuel. When the truck was full I shut off the nozzle and stepped back from his truck. The man bent over and looked down into the gas hole of his truck. Then he looked at me and pointed to the gas hole and made the cat calling sound.

Jamie – The truck is full.

He points to the hole and again makes the cat calling sound.

Jamie – The truck is full.

He points and again makes that sound.

Jamie – It's full!

I swear if right this minute I was asked if I wanted a beer or a translator I would say translator. That way, I could give this guy a good piece of my mind.

* * *

It was a pretty quiet night so I thought it would be a good idea to call Vanessa. I climb up into the cab of the truck and grab the satellite phone and dial her number. She answered the phone with much excitement in her voice. With caller ID she can tell when it's me calling. Once again I didn't have much to say. It's always hard for me to tell her how my day went because we are not allowed to tell our friends and family back home anything that goes on overseas. So once again I spent most of the time on the phone listening to her. We had been talking for about twenty minutes when I heard a pop noise off in the distance. From my location I could not see where it came from. I heard something fly over the top of my truck. Then I heard a siren and the words 'Stand-to' were shouted across the camp.

Vanessa – What was that?

I stuck my head out the door of the truck and looked up. When I did that, I heard another pop noise and something flew over the top of my truck.

Vanessa – Jamie, what is that noise?

Jamie – Vanessa, I have to let you go. Everything is okay.

She didn't want to let me go but she said goodbye and I hung up. As I placed the phone down another object flew over my head. I realized that someone was shooting rockets at my truck. We are trained to stay in the vehicle when we are shot at, but because the enemy was shooting at my truck I decided it would be better if I exited the vehicle.

The camp was surrounded by a large brick wall and my truck was parked alongside that wall. I jumped out of the truck and landed next to the wall. When I did that, machine gun fire hit along the wall. I sat there and looked up at my truck and saw another rocket go over the top. I knew if a rocket hit my truck I might not survive.

My thoughts went to Vanessa and Avery and then to Mom and Dad. I thought how crushed they would be if I died right here and now. Without a second thought I decided I would call Mom and Dad. If this was going to be my last night alive I wanted to hear their voice one more time. As I dialled their number another rocket just missed my truck. It was then I thought I was going to die, and this would be the last time I talked to my parents.

When Mom answered it was just like when Vanessa answered, with a voice so filled with excitement it made me feel like I was missed. Mom told Dad it was me on the line and he picked up the phone in his bedroom so we all could talk at once. When I heard their voices I started to get choked up and tears began to roll down my dirty face. I thought this was the last time I would ever talk to my parents.

Mom – How are you, my love?

Jamie – Don't worry about me. How are you guys doing?

They started to tell me about how they are getting ready to go to the cabin and that Dad still had a bad back but they were doing just fine.

Jamie – Mom, Dad. I want you to know that I love you very much. You guys have always been there for me for my whole life. The reason I am the man today is because of the love I received from you two.

Mom –Is everything alright, Jamie?

Jamie – Yes, Mom, everything is fine. I just wanted you guys to know how much you mean to me.

Dad – We know you love us, buddy. And we are very proud to call you our son.

Jamie – I know you are, Dad, and I'm proud to have you guys as parents.

We said our goodbyes and I hung up the phone. Then I sat there waiting for more rockets to be fired. I looked around the camp and there were LAVs running and prepared to fire. The problem was they could not identify where the enemy was located. Our orders as Canadians are that we cannot shoot at the enemy unless we can identify the target. But it was dark and no one could see where the shots were coming from, so I had to sit there and hope not to get hit. In the end, the enemy fired seven rockets and some machine gun fire, all at me, but never hit me, and we didn't fire anything back.

* * *

The next day, the camp Master Warrant Officer (MWO) came to me to see how I was doing. I told him I would be okay and that I was not hurt. Later that day I found out that the MWO had passed it on to everyone in the camp to leave me alone unless they really needed fuel. He thought I might be a little stressed. When I heard that, I thought I would have a little fun. A few hours later, a soldier pulled up in a vehicle looking for some fuel. I was lying on my cot relaxing. I heard him pull up but decided not to even raise my head from the cot. The soldier walked over to me and softly asked me for some fuel. I jumped up from my bunk and shouted:

Jamie – OH, YOU WANT SOME FUEL DO YOU? WELL, LET'S JUST GET WHAT YOU WANT, EH!

Soldier – I'm sorry. I didn't mean to disturb you. I will come back later.

I started to laugh.

Jamie – No worries. I was just kidding.

I then walked over to his vehicle with him and gave him the fuel he needed.

Well, today is a good day. Today is the day I head back to the main camp. In just three more days I am on a flight back home. Soon I will get to see my loved ones again. How I long to see Vanessa again. How good it will be to go to Mom and Dad's cabin.

The convoy back to the camp went without any problems, and the boys once again were there waiting for me. But this time they were not there to see if I was okay. This time they were there to celebrate since I was the last of the brothers to be off camp. Now that I was back the brotherhood was complete and ready to go home.

That night, I looked forward to a good night sleep, knowing that I've got tomorrow and then the day after that I am on a plane and out of this place. But just like every other night I had another nightmare. This time there were Afghan people in Mom and Dad's house and they had my parents held hostage. In the dream I could hear my father screaming in pain. And then I woke up in my bunk.

* * *

In the morning we had to head over to the church for an O group. This O group was given to each soldier before they headed back to Canada. They told us once we get home it was normal to notice that things are different. They told us that if we end up having any problems when we get back we should not bottle our feelings up. They said there were people we could see who would help us with any problems that might arise. They told us some people turn to drugs, some to booze, and others have anger problems. War affects different people in different ways.

This O group at the church took us all the way up to lunch time. After lunch, we were free to do what we wanted. Some people went for a drive around the camp for one last look. Others walked down to the PX to pick up a few items before we jumped on a plane. The rest of us sat around and played some Xbox 360. I guess we were tired of doing stuff. We just wanted to sit and enjoy the day and so that's what we did.

It's now six in the evening and we are standing on the runway waiting for the big beautiful Hercules plane that is going to take us out of here. Usually I hate getting on these things because I know it will be a long loud trip, but today it was my pleasure to get aboard.

The plane's engines were running as I took my seat and put on my seatbelt. I look around and see many smiling faces just like me. Everyone was as excited as me to lift off the ground.

The doors close and within minutes our tires are rolling and we are on the move. We quickly gain speed and I could actually feel the plane lift off the ground. All the soldiers in the plane begin to cheer as we started our long journey home.

Our plane was coming in for a landing in Edmonton, Alberta, but this was no ordinary landing. Before our landing we were met by two fighter jets that guided us in. It was really cool to see the jets coming up into the sky to meet us. It made us feel important.

All the soldiers were now in the Edmonton airport and were standing in line going through Customs. Sergeant Winchester was about twenty soldiers ahead of me. He was having his bags checked by one of the airport personnel. The person doing the checking was an East Indian and when he finished what he was doing he looked at the sergeant.

Airport personnel – Welcome to my country!

When Sergeant Winchester heard the man say that he lost control and angrily responded that it was his country first. It was wrong and can't be excused. But Sergeant Winchester's job during our tour was cleaning out vehicles after they'd been hit by IEDs or suicide bombers, cleaning out the body parts and blood of our guys after they had been killed. It was a job that only he did. He never wanted us around the damaged vehicles. His was an awful job and it continues to haunt him.

* * *

Once our bags were checked we headed out to the meeting area where we were met by many members of the Royal Canadian Legion. I stopped and shook hands with every single one of them.

There were no family members at the airport. A bus picked us up and transported us to CFB Edmonton. The bus ride was the best I had ever been on and that was because the police force in Edmonton knew the route the bus would be taking to get us to the base and had road blocks set up at every street light. That way, nothing could stop us from getting to the base as soon as possible. I never got to thank those cops, but that really meant a lot to all of us.

The bus pulls up to the training building and we get off and walk inside. I step through the last set of doors and into the parade square. There is a crowd of people and many flashes from cameras, but all I am looking for is Vanessa. I see soldiers hugging loved ones and others having interviews on TV. But where was Vanessa? She was all I wanted.

Then I felt something around my leg. I looked down and it was Avery. He was hugging my leg. I bent over and picked him up. He gave me the biggest hug this soldier has ever got. As I held him there I looked through the crowd and I saw her. My angel, my heart, my light who got me through the darkness of Afghanistan. Vanessa!

I started to walk towards her, pushing people out of my way and still carrying Avery. I saw her smile and the bigger her smile got the faster I moved until I had her in my arms. I thought Avery had hugged me hard but that was before Vanessa hugged me. She hugged hard and it felt great. To finally hold her in my arms again was all I needed in this world.

I leaned back and just looked at her, looked at her eyes, her smile. God, I love this woman.

Vanessa – Well, soldier, what do you have to say?

I looked at Avery and said, 'Daddy's home.'

After The Tour

When I got home the first thing I did was go to the fridge and thanks to good friends there was beer in my fridge. I opened one and walked to the couch and sat down. It was quiet, everyone had gone home and for now it was just me and my wonderful couch. I think about turning on the TV but I decide to enjoy the quiet for a minute. It's good not to hear people asking me questions or talking along side of me.

After a few minutes pass I decide to turn on the TV to see what is on. I don't really care what's on because I am pretty sure that it will be new to me, I have six months of TV shows to catch up on.

In my living room there is a large window facing out into the street the runs along my house. Light shines on me as a car passes. I feel a cold sweat start to form on my skin, I feel like there are eyes watching me through that window. I quickly stand up and close the blinds so people can't see in. As if there was a sniper out there with his cross hairs on me, I could not open them again.

When I finish my beer I decide to go brush my teeth, I have not done it since the flight. Standing there I realize how nice it is to be able to have privacy in the bathroom. To have no half naked man standing next to me using the sink next to mine. It was just me.

I heard a knock at the door, I don't move. The knock happens again, I still don't move. No matter whom it is I don't want to see them, I don't want to see anyone. The knocks stop, I go back to my brushing my teeth.

I decide it's time for me to go to sleep. I strip off all my clothes except for my boxers, shut off the light and climb into bed. Something was wrong, I needed to hear the outside, and I jumped from my bed and opened the window. I could hear the sounds of the cars passing; off in the distance I can hear a police car siren. The sound reminds me back to the sound of an ambulance, I suddenly think back to the medic vehicle that was on fire and the soldier that burned alive. I shake my head and climb back into bed.

After two hours of tossing and turning I finally fell asleep, but I found no comfort in sleep because this would begin my nightmares. Tonight I dreamed that my friends and I were under a gas attack. I remember we were all running trying to escape the gas. I remember running and running but never being able to out the gas. It just kept getting closer and closer to me no matter how fast I ran. I could hear my friends' screaming as the gas was burning their skin. I breathing harder and harder, the gas was right next to me and suddenly...I was awake.

The next three days we had to finish off paper work at the battalion and get checked over by the medics and talk to a head doctor, I told them whatever they wanted to hear, I just wanted out of there. All I wanted was to get some well deserved time off and relax on leave.

After the three days of getting checked and having to talk to people I finally signed my leave pass and I was out the door.

I find myself with very little patience, I noticed this when I left the base and headed to the grocery store for some food. It felt so different walking through a grocery store again. The first thing I notice is the cool air conditioning when I walk inside. There is some soft music playing through the speakers. I grab myself a cart and begin to walk up and down the aisles picking out things I wanted in my kitchen.

It wasn't too long and my cart was filled, so I headed to the check out. But when I got there I found many people already there waiting in line.

My heart started to beat faster, my palms became very sweaty as I gripped the handle of the grocery cart tight. I knew that if I went up there I would be surrounded by people I didn't know, and how long would I have to wait there. It just wasn't worth it, so I left the cart there and walked back out to my truck.

Vanessa came later that night with groceries for me; she packed my fridge and opened my curtains. As much as I hated the curtains open because people could look in at me I didn't say anything.

Vanessa asked me how my day was, but I didn't want to tell her. I was afraid of what she would think of me. I decided to tell her about the good parts of my day, but every time I would say a few words, she would cut me off with another question. Each time she cut me off I could feel this heat building in my body, it wasn't just anger, and it was like I was being possessed by someone else. I found myself wanting to hurt Vanessa. But not in a physical way, but in a mental way, I wanted to hurt her feelings.

I started to say things to Vanessa that I knew would hurt her, it was like I wanted her to cry, I wanted her to get mad at me and have a fight with me. Every word I shouted felt like ecstasy, because it felt so good to shout at her I kept doing it. We shouted back and forth until she could take no more and she walked out, and again, I am alone.

For the next two weeks I stay downstairs in the rec room. For one, the temperature was a lot cooler there and after being where I have been the cool air was a welcome change. Another reason why I was downstairs was because I didn't want to see anyone. Well anyone except Vanessa, but I could tell I wasn't ready to see her. If I could be mean to her I could be mean to anyone, so I barricaded myself in the basement.

Days would pass and I would hear knocks at the front door and the back. Sometimes people would walk up to the window and look inside. I would sneak upstairs and take a peek to see who it was. But I wasn't really hiding, my truck was still parked outside, I just wanted away from the world until I was ready to deal with the world and the new me.

* * *

I have been home in Edmonton for about two weeks now and for the most part I have spent that time in the basement watching TV. A lot of soldiers spend their time off with family or doing a lot of drinking. Who really knows why; everyone is different and everyone handles things different. I wanted to be alone. When I was growing up I spent a lot of time by myself and the reason for that was because there weren't many children my age around Mom and Dad's cabin and we were there often. I guess because I spent so much time alone when I was younger it wasn't that much different to what I was doing now. It felt better to be by myself right now. I didn't want to be around people.

My parents really wanted me to come back to Newfoundland for a trip. It's funny. When I was overseas in Afghanistan all I wanted to do was return to Newfoundland and see all my family again. But when I got back from Afghanistan, I didn't want to go to Newfoundland. It's like I was just not ready to see my family. Maybe it's because I know I have changed and I know they are expecting the same old guy they remember. But I'm not that guy anymore. Maybe I'm not ready to go back to Newfoundland because I know reporters are going to want to interview me about my experiences in Afghanistan. I know many people back home are going to have questions and I just don't want to have to deal with that.

Part of me is just scared to be around people. It seems like I end up getting upset with anyone I am around and I start to say rude things to them. It seems too that the more important the person is to me the ruder I am. Poor Vanessa. I love her so much but I have said so many rude things to her in the past few weeks. So far she has stuck by my side. I don't deserve her.

Every night I have a nightmare and it's really starting to affect me during the day. Because I am not sleeping at night I am tired all day. And being tired all through the day has made it harder to control my anger.

After a few weeks of me being locked in the basement, Vanessa invited me out to dinner with her and her mother. Vanessa's parents split up when she was fourteen so her mom lives alone. Used to be that when I was told we were going out to dinner I would get excited. But when Vanessa gave me the news about going out to dinner with her and her mother I quickly became nervous. It was just like I had been told I had an appointment with the dentist. I kept thinking about the dinner date all week and dreading it.

The dinner was on a Saturday night so that day Vanessa came over to hang out before we headed out. Nowadays I don't have much to say, but I do listen, so Vanessa did most of the talking. We talked about moving in together and I thought that was a great idea. Maybe having her around will help me break out of my shell.

But I told her before she moved in with me there are a few things she needs to know. I told her I had weapons hidden all through my house, not guns, but knives, baseball bats and police batons. I told her how I feel like there are people out there who want to hurt me. I told her how I find it so hard to relax, my guard is always up. The army taught me how to switch on my soldier mode. Problem is they don't teach you how to switch it off.

Vanessa took my hand and looked me in the eye and told me everything would be okay. She told me she knows what she is getting into by being with a war vet. She said whatever we are faced with we will face it together, and she told me she will always be there for me. Her words made me feel so good. It was wonderful to know there was someone willing to stand behind me no matter what happens, to know that I had someone I could always count on. It was then I realized that I wanted to spend the rest of my life with her.

Vanessa picked me up Saturday evening. When she walked in through the front door she asked me why I had all the blinds closed. She said it was a beautiful day and I should let the sun come in. I told her I had them closed because I can't sit comfortably in the house thinking that people might be able to see me. I said maybe it was because I spent so much time worrying about snipers or people trying to attack me while I was in Afghanistan. I said now for my own peace of mind I keep the blinds closed.

On the drive to the restaurant I wanted to tell Vanessa about how I had been nervous all day long thinking about going out to dinner with her and her mom. But being the big and tough soldier it was hard for me to show weakness or to tell her I was having these feelings.

When we pulled into the parking lot the first thing I noticed was how many vehicles were parked there. I didn't like crowds so seeing all these vehicles made me very uncomfortable. I could feel my palms getting sweaty, a trait that that was passed down to me by my father.

As soon as I stepped in through the front door of the restaurant it was like all my soldier instincts kicked in. I immediately looked for all the exits so that I could plan my escape route in case something happened.

A greeter took us to the table where Vanessa's mother was already sitting waiting for us. Vanessa and I sat on one side of the table. Vanessa's mother and her boyfriend sat across from us. Throughout the entire meal I didn't have much to say. I was mostly answering questions about my tour. Vanessa's mother and her boyfriend were very curious about what I did over in Afghanistan, but I wasn't ready to tell anyone about that.

I had a very hard time focusing on what was going on at our table because I was so busy checking out everyone else in the restaurant. I would size up every guy in the building, wondering if they were good at fighting and whether or not they would give me trouble if I had to take them out. If someone looked suspicions to me I would really look hard at them so I would be able to give a description of them if I had to.

Then something bad happened. A waiter behind me opened a bottle of wine. When he popped the cork out of the bottle there was a loud popping sound. When I heard it my whole body went cold. My breathing started to pick up. Vanessa noticed and she took my hand and could feel its cold clamminess. She asked me if I was okay. I just nodded yes, embarrassed to tell her the truth. It was hard, but I made it through the night and made it back home.

That night, I had another nightmare. In this one Vanessa was kidnapped while she was in her own car. I remember her car getting further and further away from me no matter how fast I was going in my car. When I woke up Vanessa was sitting up in the bed next to me. Turns out I was screaming her name in my sleep.

* * *

I was now halfway through my leave and I knew I had to go back to Newfoundland for a visit. I thought it would be good for me to see family and old friends again. The army paid for my flight. When I landed in Deer Lake there were many family members there waiting to see me. It felt so good to know that all these people had come. Maybe this is what I needed. My mother could not stop hugging me, and I loved every minute of it. Although my trip home would only be a week long it was better than no trip at all.

While I was home I had the media at my parents' door asking to do interviews and take pictures. If it wasn't a reporter at my door it was some company dropping off something to say thank you for my service in Afghanistan. A representative from the local Coca-Cola Company came to the door with hats, shirts and cases of Coke for me. Tim Horton's showed up with donuts for the family. Molson showed up with free beer. Dad loved every minute of it because of the free stuff.

Throughout the week my family could tell that I had changed and they didn't really understand why. They kind of knew what I had gone through overseas but they still couldn't understand why I was acting the way I was.

I had no patience anymore. Small things made me mad and I would show my anger by yelling or leaving the room. It was like I could not control what I was saying. Like I wanted to hurt people because I was hurting. I was so negative towards everything and everyone. With my family, if you're acting like an ass you will be told, and I was told. But when I was confronted about the way I was acting I could not tell them why I was acting this way. And because I could not explain myself to my family it made things very difficult.

After the final confrontation with my family I spent the last days of my trip in my old bedroom, all alone. I was afraid to be around my family because I didn't want to say the wrong thing and make things worse. I stayed in the house with my mother and father up until it was time for me to fly back to Edmonton. At the airport, I hugged them both and said goodbye. I told them I would see them soon. But at that time I didn't know if I would ever come back.

Now that my leave was over it was time for me to head back to work. I hated the thought of putting my uniform back on but I knew I had to. It was weird putting on a green uniform after spending so much time in a tan one over in Afghanistan. Over my leave I often thought about leaving the army, about maybe finding something new to work at. But the thought of trying something new scares me. I have been with the army since I was old enough to work. It's all I know.

* * *

For the first week back at work I was mostly walking around the building saying hello to people I have not seen for months. It was good to see everyone again. They all asked how my tour was and how I was doing. I was too embarrassed to tell them I was doing so badly, that I was angry all the time, that I can't sleep at night, and when I do my night is filled with nightmares.

Weeks turn into months and I am not getting any better. I find myself losing my cool at least once a day. When I get angry I find it helps if I go outside and walk around the compound where all our vehicles are kept. I find the fresh cool air calms me down.

While I was overseas I became used to taking my weapon with me everywhere I went. Now, when I am at work I find myself always thinking I forgot my weapon. I move a vehicle from one place to another and when I get out and take a few steps away from the vehicle I have a little panic attack because I think I have lost my weapon.

Today at work we did some convoy operations training, which is practicing driving in a convoy and then the convoy gets attacked. Well, when our convoy got attacked in the training it was my vehicle that was hit. Once my vehicle was hit I grabbed my rifle and jumped out of the cab of the truck.

For this training they had soldiers dressed up like Afghan people. When I saw these people it was like I was back overseas again. One of the people dressed like Afghans came up to me and when I was face to face with him, without even thinking, I quickly grabbed him, disarmed him, and slammed him to the ground. I wasn't thinking that these people were Canadians. All I could see was Taliban. This guy I put down wasn't alone. There was another guy dressed as a Taliban soldier and he came to help out the first guy, so I disarmed him and put him to the ground too.

It was at this point there was a ceasefire called on all training because of what I had done. At the end of the day it was decided that people from my tour would not be doing any more convoy operations training until they had enough time to decompress. Also I was told that I would have to start going to mental health.

It didn't go very well with the first guy I saw at mental health. He started making me feel bad for the way I was acting and implied it was my fault that I am angry all the time. I remember yelling at him and being asked to leave. But somehow I did stick with it. I looked at it as something I was doing for Vanessa. She didn't deserve the person I have become. All I wanted to do was argue. I wanted to fight people who were my friends.

For three months I saw the same guy in mental health, and I thought he might actually be helping me through all of this. But just when I started to think this was working the army posted the guy to another province in Canada. So with him gone I had to start anew with someone else. This time, they put me with a licensed shrink and this doctor and I did not see eye to eye. We would get together once a week to talk about how my week was going. Always, at the end of each session, she would tell me she wanted me to try these pills. Always with the pills. Just like overseas, they wanted us to take pills to help keep us calm. Or to keep the pain in check until the mission was complete. I have seen guys from my tour get hooked on pills and now it's like they need them. But what happens when the pills run out? I guess they turn to the bottle.

* * *

Another night has come and gone and I hardly slept again. 'Why don't you think you're sleeping?' That's the question I am asked by my head doctor. Well, where do I begin? Let's start with the nightmares. Last night I had a dream that my son was kidnapped. I remember driving after the black van he was in and no matter how fast I drove the van would just get further and further away from me.

I wake up and I am covered with sweat. I sit up and look around, knowing now that I will never get back to sleep. I look down at Vanessa. She is lying there quietly, and now I am angry with her because she can sleep the night away and I am lucky to get three hours in a row. I used to be able to wake up and roll over and fall back to sleep in minutes. Now, when I wake up, it's like my mind won't shut off, and I am up for hours.

With very little sleep I now become even easier to make angry.

Before my tour in Afghanistan, I used to love going to a party, loved going out to eat or going to a club for a few drinks. Meeting people was one of my things I enjoyed. I wanted to make as many friends as I could. Now, I don't even want to answer the phone when it rings. I no longer want to go out to eat. I don't want to be around people I don't know. I just don't trust people anymore, so how can I be around them when I always think they are out to get me.

Sometimes I wonder if it's because I worry too much about what people think of me or what people are saying about me. I know the tour has changed who I was and I don't want people to know or think I have changed.

I find it so hard to go anywhere. Everything seems like an effort. It's hard to sit in a restaurant and enjoy my food when I am constantly looking over my shoulder thinking someone might try to rob the place. I look at people sitting at other tables and size them up so I could give a description of them if necessary. I check to see where the exits are and plan what I would do if someone tried to rob the place. I make a plan in my head on how to get Vanessa and the kids kids out safely. My mind never relaxes. I always have to have a plan in case the worst thing happens.

* * *

For over two years I have been seeing a head doctor, but it seems like every time I start getting close to someone, the army posts them away. When I get a new head doctor I have to start all over again. It seems like every time I go to see a head doctor all they want to talk about are dangerous moments I had overseas. When I leave an appointment, I find myself very tired or in a bad mood because I just spent the last hour re-living things I would just as soon forget. Why can't we talk about what could cool me down when I get angry? No, they would rather talk about what makes me angry then give me some pills.

I get pills to help me sleep at night, and then more pills to help me stay awake during the day. It's like the army will give me what I need to get me through the day. But I don't want to be just another soldier on pills. I need to find a way to beat this myself. I know what I need. Dad and Mom's cabin.

The cabin where I grew up, that's where I forget the stress and the problems. I love to walk out to the water and listen to the water flow. Sometimes you can hear a passing loon or see a moose walk out to the water to get a drink. I could sit there for hours and watch the world go by.

I spent two years going in and out of mental health places only to find out that going to these classes made me even more angry. Talking about my anger just made me angry. So when you think nothing is going to help your anger, you try and learn to live with it. You learn to know the things that make you mad, and the things that calm you down. Cool air always calmed me down. I would find myself going for long walks to cool off at times. Many times at work I would leave the building and walk around outside trying to calm down.

I have learned to live with my anger so well that it has become a part of me, it is my darkness within. Once my darkness takes control I am no longer myself, and I have no control over what I say or what I do. I can see everything that is happening, but I can't control what's happening and that scares me.

My anger really became a problem. I found myself yelling at Avery and Vanessa a lot. At times I wondered if I was trying to pick a fight with them because I needed to yell at someone.

There was a time in my life when I liked the anger. It felt good to become angry because I felt stronger when I was angry. I felt tough, like nothing could hurt me.

I started to get nervous about going anywhere. I hated to be around anyone I didn't know. I thought everyone was out to get me. At my house, I had police batons hidden in places where I could find them in case someone broke into the house. My mind was never at rest. At night, when I tried to sleep my mind was filled with nightmares. One thing was always the same about my nightmares. They were always about one of my family members in trouble and me trying to get to them before they are killed.

I would wake up from the nightmare and look at the clock. 1:45

Go back to sleep and wake again, look at the clock. 3:30

I would keep waking up every one or two hours. It was like I was scared I was going to be late for work. I have heard of people not being able to sleep because they are excited about starting a new job, but for me it was every night. Getting very little sleep made it even easier for me to become angry.

I explain to Avery that his dad is like the Incredible Hulk. When the Bruce Banner character gets angry he turns into the Hulk, and when he is the Hulk he can't really control what he does. He can only feel sorry for what is done.

I find myself in an argument with Vanessa almost every day, and half of them I don't even know why we are fighting. I just know that after we fight and I walk away and have time to think about it I end up feeling bad for what I have said. It seems like the little things make me mad and when I start to yell it is so hard to stop. It's like holding in your pee for a very long time and once you start you just don't want to stop. That's how I feel when I start to yell.

I am not sleeping at night because of my nightmares and this does not help my moods. My lack of sleep has made it easier to get mad.

I started staying at the homes of friends and avoiding Vanessa because it felt like we were always in a fight. But my late nights stopped when I came home and found Vanessa with a bag packed and carrying Avery out the front door. I begged her to stay and to give me one more chance. There were tears in both our eyes when she agreed to stay. After that, I stayed home.

* * *

One day I was out driving in my truck and I had to stop for fuel. I pulled into a gas station and proceeded to fill my truck. But what I didn't realize was that I was using a pre-pay pump. So I got out of my truck and I placed the nozzle in and waited for the guy inside to turn on the pump. After five minutes passed I start to wonder what is taking him so long to turn it on. As I wait there I can feel my face getting hot and my anger building.

So I started to walk inside and before I made it to the door a woman met me halfway and let me know that I was using a pre-pay pump. When I looked back I saw there was a sign saying that but the sign was low on the pump and I had not seen it before. So I said sorry to the lady and I was going to go inside to pay for the gas first. She told me not to worry about it. She said she would turn on the pump. I thanked her and proceeded to fill my tank.

When I got inside the gas station there was a long line so I stood at the end and waited for my turn. Behind the counter was a guy and there was a woman working the cash and also the woman I spoke to outside. I could hear the guy calling me a dummy for not being able to see the sign on the pump.

His words brought my anger to a peak. When I got to the cash I stared at him. I wasn't thinking anything. It was like I was in a daze. Then suddenly I snapped and I said to him:

"The reason I didn't see the sign is because you put it very low to the ground. I don't know if you meant to have the sign at eye level for children. And let me tell you something else. For saying that I am a dummy I feel like grabbing you and pulling you across the counter and tossing you through that plate glass window."

The man turned red and started to say something, and then I spoke again. "Save it, pal. But you had better pray I don't see you on the streets any time because by the time I am done with you you will be a dummy for life."

And I then stormed out of the gas station.

Anger

When we went overseas to Afghanistan it was like this switch was turned off in my head. It was like I knew the danger that was out there and I knew that it could strike at anytime. I knew that you could not identify your enemy so there was no way to see an attack coming. So I turned off the switch to my feelings. When you are in danger you don't think about the bad that could happen; you just concentrate on the mission and completing it.

You don't think about that guy with a bomb strapped to his chest, waiting for you to drive by so he can run up and end both of your lives. Or about that guy with a gun off in the distance with his cross hairs trained on your head.

As a trucker, you just keep driving. You black out the bad and just drive.

The problem is that when you block out your fears and your feelings it's so hard to get them back. When a fellow soldier falls in battle we are expected to soldier on. We cry on each other's shoulders, and we become a family. We become brothers.

As brothers we soldier on and complete the mission. If you act like everyone is a possible Taliban soldier you would drive yourself crazy. So you forget about the IEDs and you just drive. Even though you have seen so many IEDs take out other vehicles you push the fear away and drive.

At the beginning of the tour, if you heard a rocket attack on the camp you might have got a little frightened and ran for cover. But soon you stop running and you sit and light a smoke to watch the show. You watch the people scatter and jump into bunkers. But you don't jump into any bunker because after what you have seen out on the road, this rocket attack on the camp is a joke.

At first when people shot at you, you would duck and start to sweat. But after it happens so many times it makes you angry that someone is shooting at you even though you are over here in their country trying to help.

After so many things happen to you it becomes harder to sleep. Could this be the night that the Taliban fire a good shot and hits my tent, maybe even hits me? It could happen, so you try and put it out of your mind. It becomes another thing to try and block out. After a while of having to block out so many things it's hard to judge what is good from bad and what is right from wrong.

Overseas you get so angry because you see people being hurt and you can't do anything about it. You see rape victims, mostly young boys. It makes you think of kids you know back home and you get so mad that people are getting away with this all the time. It gets to the point where you don't want anyone to get away with anything bad anymore.

When you are faced with a situation in Afghanistan you only know one way to handle it and that's with speed and directness. If that becomes second nature for you it makes it hard when you come home. Because that is not the way to handle things when you come back home. In Afghanistan you didn't always have time to think, you could only react, but at home you have to learn to think before you do anything.

So they tell you have anger problems and that you have post traumatic stress syndrome. Well, no wonder you have anger problems. You're up all night because you can't sleep from all the nightmares. You don't want to be around anyone because most times you end up not liking something they said and you end up yelling and attacking them verbally.

Then they send you to a head doctor who wants to talk about your feelings and what makes you angry. When all you want to say to the doctor is that talking to him/her is what makes you angry. What, are you working on another book, Doc? Shouldn't we work on what makes me calm instead of what makes me angry? Nope, you just want me to take a pill to help me sleep. But then that pill makes me tired in the daytime. So I have to take another to keep me going. The next thing you know you have so many pills you don't even know what they do anymore. Head doctors don't help today's soldier. Most soldiers want to forget what they have seen and move on with their lives.

If I could give advice to the people out there with anger problems I would tell them that every person is different and every tour is different. Don't be ashamed of how you're feeling. If you're angry like me, find what calms you down and use it. It could be anything from a long walk with time to think or maybe you need to have someone there to talk to. Don't be afraid to get the help you need. There are a lot of good programs out there with lots of good people waiting to listen. Or maybe what you need is the love of a good family. That's what works for me. I love having my beautiful wife and two boys to come home to; they are my whole world.

I remember once I was asked why I wanted to fight for my country overseas? My answer was: When you work with and train for war with people for so long you become like family, like brothers, and how could I let my brothers go off to fight without me? Now that I am a father I have another reason to add to my answer. I fight so my children won't have too. I will soldier on. And will this soldier fight again? If his country asks him too, he will always say yes.

Love and Marriage

I had the feeling that Vanessa was thinking of leaving me and giving up on us. Who could blame her? I have not been the easiest person to live with. Even though I have learned some methods to help keep me calm I have not done a very good job of keeping my anger in check.

No matter how I acted I loved Vanessa and I did not want to lose her. I decided I wanted to ask her to marry me so I went out and found me a ring I thought my Vanessa would love. I had it hid away in the bedroom until I could think of a good way to propose to her.

One night, I got a call from Julian Austin, the country singer I had met in Afghanistan. We chatted for awhile and I told him I was going to ask Vanessa to marry me. He started to laugh and said that he would be playing a coming home concert at Rexhall Place in Edmonton and it would be a great idea for me to propose to Vanessa on stage in front of an audience of thousands of people.

At first I didn't like the idea because I thought, 'What if she says no?' But then I thought that this would be something to remember forever. The night of the concert I took Vanessa backstage to meet Julian and we chatted and talked to Vanessa about how we met overseas. But within minutes of our chatting he had to go onstage and start playing.

Vanessa and I were standing to the far left of the stage. Vanessa had no idea I had spoken to Julian earlier and the plan was that he would sing two songs and then invite me on stage to do my thing. After the two songs were finished I heard Julian call me up on stage. That's when I took Vanessa by the hand and led her on stage in front of thousands and asked her to spend the rest of her life with me. Vanessa didn't hesitate. She smiled her beautiful smile and said 'Yes' and the crowd cheered wildly. It was a moment I will always remember. Not long afterwards, I made our family whole when I adopted Avery as my son.

Our wedding took place in Corner Brook, Newfoundland. It was the first military wedding Corner Brook had seen in a long time. Standing by my side were my brother and guys that I had called my best friends at some point in my life. Vanessa wore a beautiful red wedding dress. I lost my breath when I watched her walk down the aisle and stand by my side. I wondered how a woman so beautiful could choose me to spend the rest of her life with. I was the luckiest man alive.

After the wedding ceremony, we walked out through the front doors of the church and there were World War II veterans holding up swords for Vanessa and me to walk under. I was so proud to have these great men be a part of such a wonderful moment in my life. It just goes to show that no matter what the age all soldiers are brothers.

If you're wondering how was our wedding night, well, to tell you the truth, our next child was conceived that night. Weeks later in Edmonton when we found out how far along Vanessa was we did the math and, sure enough, the baby was conceived on our wedding night.

Nine months later Vanessa gave birth to Cody Douglas. We named him Douglas after my father. Reason one you name your son after a great man is because you want him to turn out just like the great man. Reason two for me was because the greatest man I know is my father. He, just like my mother, Kay, never tried to rule my life. Dad and Mom guided me and, most importantly, they always stood behind me. I hope I can now give my children as good a childhood as they gave me.

I served at the Battalion in Edmonton for five more years. I kept going to mental health once a week. I thought it would be for the best. If I did end up losing it and hitting someone at work at least they could see that I was trying. Ha ha ha.

But those five years were not easy. For three of those years I had nightmares every night. And for two years I would wake up with no memory of any dream. Through those years Vanessa and I had many fights. It was mostly because of me coming home from work angry and taking it out on her. And I often lost it when the children left toys out in the living room. Seemed like I was always yelling at someone when I first got home from work. I was an angry driver as well and had no problem chasing after someone I thought did me wrong on the road.

In the year 2010, I got the news that my parents had been waiting years for. I was posted to St John's, Newfoundland. I was going home. Well, maybe not to Corner Brook, but it was back on the Rock.

Avery was very excited. He had been on trips to Newfoundland with us before and he loved every minute of being there. My parents loved spoiling him and their new grandson, little Cody. Avery got to go to the cabin and do all the things I had done when I was his age: fish, swim in the river, have a camp fire. We did all of those things together and I found they brought us together as a family. I now understand why my father had done all of those things with his kids. It made his family tighter.

Now that we are living in Newfoundland, my family and I have taken many trips to Mom and Dad's cabin. I think every time I go there I feel a little less angry. Even Vanessa says I am a different man when we are at the cabin. She said I have never raised my voice there. So we go there as often as we can. Avery likes to fish and Cody, well, he is like his old man. He likes to drive vehicles! He and I are on his grandfather's Quad bike whenever we are at the cabin. I guess it's all about how I'm making myself and my family stronger. Vanessa is great. And as for me? How am I doing? Well, I'm soldiering on.

There was a time in my life when I thought I would never be rid of my anger. That was until I held Cody in my arms for the first time. I can't explain what I felt then, but the best way I can say it is just one word. Peace.

Cody is now four, and Avery is ten. And Vanessa and I couldn't be happier. A few years after our wedding I got posted to Newfoundland. I don't get paid quite as much for being back on The Rock but I don't care. It's worth it to be able to drive to Mom and Dad's cabin. To see Dad playing with my sons and Mom baking them cookies is worth more to me than the world. I have found my reason for going on and my reason for keeping control of my darkness and that reason is my family. From time to time I do have outbursts but who doesn't? I am able to control them now, and my love for my family and their love for me has never been stronger, and I am stronger for it.

I used to take pills to help me sleep and I was on antidepressants for a while. I even had a pill I could put under my tongue for when I would get really angry. But I haven't taken any pills since my posting back to Newfoundland. Getting back to the island where I grew up was all the medicine I needed.

Epilogue

In 2013, Afghanistan remains Canada's largest overseas military commitment with some 950 Canadian soldiers and 45 civilian police deployed as part of a NATO mission to train Afghan soldiers and police. Canada's Foreign Affairs Stabilization and Reconstruction Task Force will spend about $25 million a year in Afghanistan until 2014, when the military mission is due to end.

To date, more than 150 Canadian soldiers have been killed in Afghanistan and 2,000 wounded, many disabled for life. The figure for those wounded does not include the thousands of Candians soldiers suffering from post-traumatic stress and other psychological damage. A recent Defence department study predicted up to 13.2 per cent of the 40,000 Canadian soldiers who served in Afghanistan could be suffering such injuries. And there are thousands more who are, or will be, seeking professional help for other combat related mental disorders, such as depression or general anxiety. According to Veterans Affairs Canada, 6,732 Afghan veterans were receiving disability benefits as of October 1, 2011.

Shocking stories of Taliban prisoners being handed over to Afghan authorities by Canadian troops and subsequently tortured became public in 2007. The matter so rocked the Canadian political world that it threatened to topple Harper's minority government in late 2009, a fate the Conservatives avoided by shutting down Parliament.

According to a 2010 poll, a majority of Canadians believed the Taliban prisoners had been tortured after they were turned over to Afghan authorities. But those polled saw the matter as a chain of command issue where responsibility rested at the top and not with individual soldiers. In June of 2012, the Military Police Complaints Commission, in a long-awaited report, concluded Canadian military police officers had no grounds to open an investigation into the treatment of suspected Taliban prisoners after they were handed over to local authorities in Kandahar. The commission concluded the cops had been kept in the dark.

* * *

From its capital in Kandahar, the Taliban ruled as the Islamic Emirate of Afghanistan from September 1996 to December 2001. Today, more than a decade after its government was brought down, the Taliban continue to operate as an insurgent force in Afghanistan.

On January 2, 2013, The Telegraph newspaper reported the number of Afghan soldiers killed fighting the Taliban had increased by one fifth as NATO forces withdrew and local troops faced the brunt of the still continuing war. The Afghan National Army (ANA) is now 17,000 strong and of that number 1,050 Afghan troops died in 2012. Meanwhile, NATO deaths have continued to fall. As of January 1, 2013, a total of 1, 405 coalition troops had been killed in the Afghan campaign in 2012, down from 566 in 2011 and 711 in 2010, according to the icasualties monitoring website.

From the time of the invasion in 2001 up until January of 2013 there have been a total of 3,253 coalition fatalities. For the same period, the American Department of Defense estimates Taliban deaths at more than 30,000, al-Qaeda at more than 2,500, Afghan government forces at 6,100 and Afghan civilians at 34,000. These figures do not include the thousands and thousands of military personnel and civilians who have been left wounded physically and mentally, many of them disabled for life.

Jamie's Photo Album

My first convoy

Me

My home in Camp Martello

Scenes from Afghanistan

When this picture was taken we were told it would be used on television and in newspapers or magazines in the event we were killed.

Left to right: Anthony Aucoin, Vincent Burgess, Mark Pinsent, Darren Fudge, Me, Daniel Flynn.

An IED we found under our truck

We buried my fuel truck in Martello
to hide from enemy fire

Singer Julian Austin at Canada House. I went from being a fan to being a good friend